JUL'1🌑 *—Sept.10=4*

STORYTELLING

STORYTELLING:
BEWITCHING THE MODERN MIND

◆

CHRISTIAN SALMON

TRANSLATED BY
DAVID MACEY

VERSO
London • New York

Ouvrage publié avec le concours du Ministère français chargé de la
culture — Centre national du livre
This work was published with the help of the French Ministry of
Culture — Centre national du livre

English edition published by Verso 2010
© Verso 2010
First published as
Storytelling: La machine à fabriquer des histoires et à formater les esprits
© Éditions La Découverte, Paris 2007

1 3 5 7 9 10 8 6 4 2

Verso
UK: 6 Meard Street, London W1F 0EG
US: 20 Jay Street, Suite 1010, Brooklyn, NY 11201
www.versobooks.com

Verso is the imprint of New Left Books

ISBN-13: 978-1-84467-391-9

British Library Cataloguing in Publication Data
A catalogue record for this book is available from the British Library

Library of Congress Cataloging-in-Publication Data
A catalog record for this book is available from the Library of Congress

Typeset by MJ Gavan, Truro, Cornwall
Printed in the US by Worldcolor / Fairfield

Contents

Preface to the English-Language Edition

During his period of exile in Rome, Gogol constantly begged his women friends back home in Russia to send him stories: stories about peasants and bureaucrats, stories about civil servants and money-lenders, and anecdotes from everyday life, to use in the second volume of *Dead Souls*, which he never completed. "Give your naïve stories to the world," he begged in his letters. The formula makes us laugh, but our era has made it its own. The injunction to tell stories has swollen to become a popular obsession, an ideology and even a slogan—the slogan for a whole era. Managers tell their employees to tell stories. The big brands urge consumers to tell stories. "Tell stories" is the cry that is used to rally soldiers who are undergoing training. Spin doctors advise politicians to tell stories. Stories are invading newspaper columns, legal arguments, and computer screens.

This book is the product of an investigation into the new ways that narratives are being used in areas as diverse as management, marketing, political and institutional communications, and the manufacture of news —and into the surprising applications of narrative in both civilian and military domains. If you decide, as I did when I began my investigations, to use a search engine to explore the immense domain of the new uses that are being made of narrative, you will discover a great diversity of techniques and uses, ranging from traditional orality to digital writing and "digital storytelling," and a plethora of practices used in management, communications, marketing, education, and therapy. There are spontaneous cultural practices, but there are also technologies of control and discipline. The Internet explosion has revolutionized the discursive economy (the production, accumulation, and circulation of discourses) and blurred the distinction between true and false, reality and fiction. A new continent is emerging. As yet, we cannot map its contours, but we can identify four main entities or regions:

1. At the microeconomic level of the company, storytelling has been incorporated into the production techniques ("storytelling management") and the sales techniques ("narrative branding") that make it possible to produce, transform, and distribute commodities. The expression refers to forms of action and control mechanisms that are designed to provide a response to a general crisis in participation and to the need to mobilize individuals on a permanent basis. These are practices that configure actual behaviors such as learning, adaptation, training, and guidance. They are used to control individuals, to manage emotional flows and affective investments, and to organize the world of sense-perceptions.

2. At the politico-ideological level, stories are used to capture people's attention, to make the actions of those who govern us look credible and to allow them to win power … The goal is to involve the masses, and to synchronize and mobilize individuals and emotions. This is the task of candidates' "spin doctors" and of the lobbies that tell their political stories. The 2008 Democratic convention in Denver supplies the model.

3. At the juridico-political level, storytelling inspires the new technologies of power that determine how individuals behave and subordinates them to certain ends through the use of surveillance, thanks to closed-circuit television, and profiling. This is the equivalent of what Michel Foucault identified and described as the "power of writing" that presided over the birth of disciplinary societies (the emergence of registers and files). In the digital age, it takes the form of a "narrative power" that can not only record the comings and goings of individuals, or what they say and do—it can now predict how they will behave and "profile" their stories.

4. At the individual level, finally, the success of blogs provides a striking example of the fad for stories. According to the Pew Research Center's Internet & American Life Project, someone starts to write a blog every second. Seventy-seven percent of bloggers are interested only in talking about "my life and experiences." The report, which was published in July 2006, is entitled "A Portrait of the Internet's New Storytellers."

How are we to interpret the stories that flow through the mediasphere?

Could they be an expression of the age-old human need to tell stories about ourselves, to identify ourselves and use narratives to give a meaning to our experiences? Has the Internet explosion provided storytelling with a new space and a readership that can be expanded to infinity? Or is it just one of those new managerial fashions that emerges every ten or fifteen years and that has now spread to the spheres of politics and the media? Do we have to see the increase in narrative profiling that allows the widespread inclusion of tracked experiences in ever more integrated databases as the menacing shadow of a new Big Brother who has traded in his old optical surveillance equipment for profiling and simulation technologies? The countless stories produced by the propaganda machine are protocols for training and domestication, and they are designed to take control of and appropriate the knowledge and desires of individuals.

Modern "storytelling" practices are not simply technologies for formatting discourses. They are also the very space within which discourses are elaborated and transmitted, a *dispositif* in which social forces and institutions, storytellers and the tellers of counter-stories, and encoding and formatting technologies, either come into conflict or collude with one another—and we must not forget the fragmented speech that constantly throbs and reverberates throughout the mediasphere. The huge accumulation of stories produced by modern societies has given birth to a "new narrative order" in which stories of power clash with stories of resistance, and have to pass the credibility test. The outcome is never decided in advance or determined by their narrative form.

Even though the second part of this book adopts a very critical stance when it looks at the ways in which narratives are explicitly used to conceal or distort the truth, and to manipulate states and public opinion (practices which became commonplace during George W. Bush's presidential term), my intention is not to liken all these narrative practices to mere propaganda, but to identify what is at stake in them, the ways in which they operate, and their specific effects.

I think that Barack Obama's election campaign proves my point. Obama turned political storytelling into a new rhetorical art. In the afterword to this edition, I trace the main stages of his campaign, which I followed week by week in the column I wrote for *Le Monde* throughout 2008. As I followed it, I became somewhat dubious, torn between an enthusiasm that was shared by most Europeans and my own doubts about the formidable storytelling machines developed by the candidate's team. I, like many of you no doubt, have yet to reach any firm conclusions.

American readers should be warned: the lines you are about to read were not written by a European expert on the United States, but by a dubious pilgrim who wandered through American realities with the wide eyes of Montesquieu's legendary Persian and the naiveté of the hero of Elia Kazan's film *America, America*.

CS
September 12, 2009

Acknowledgments

I would like to thank the video-maker Sandy Amerio for her stimulating work on storytelling; Anne Berger, Professor of French Literature at Cornell University; Philip Lewis, former Dean at Cornell, and Catherine Porter, the American translator of "French Theory," for their inspiration and hospitality during my stay in Ithaca in 2001, which is when the idea for this book was born; Jean Baudrillard for his encouragement and the interest he took in my research; Fernando Bernado, University of Coimbra, at whose seminar I first presented my research.

My thanks are due to François Gèze, *président-directeur général* of Editions La Découverte for his help in composing and writing this book and for being much more than an editor; to Marie-José Monday, who allowed me to talk about its themes more than once in her seminar. I am also grateful to her for her openness, her support, and the stimulating nature of our many exchanges.

I would also like to thanks Jean-Marie Schaeffer, Director of the Centre des recherches sur les arts et le langage, and Philippe Roussin, who heads the "Textes et littératures" research team, for welcoming me into his team and its laboratory at the CNRS. I could not be more grateful to Paul Virilio for his longstanding friendship and trust.

My thanks go, finally, to Emmanuelle Zoll, who drew my attention to many aspects of American culture and cultural globalization, such as the phenomena of acculturation in Bombay's call centers, and who was present throughout the writing of this book.

Introduction:
The Magic of Narrative, or, the
Art of Telling Stories

On the streets of a war-torn town, a group of children gathered near a football pitch warn you that there are mines in the area. A woman accuses you of murdering her husband. A man is approaching on a donkey cart: is this the individual your commanding officer suspects has been smuggling explosives? The strange lettering of the Arabic graffiti on the walls means nothing to you. How are you going to react? You have five minutes left. Your radio reminds you to act fast. You remember your mission: "Trust no one and nothing. Don't believe anything or anyone. But let them know you are there and on your guard."

This is not the screenplay for a war film. It is a video game used to train American troops to fight in Iraq. It was developed by the Institute for Creative Technologies, a research center at the University of Southern California founded by the Pentagon in 1999. Its mission is to make Hollywood's expertise available to the Pentagon so as to develop new training methods. When it was set up, for the Army Secretary Louis Caldera made no secret of the new institute's ambitions: "This will revolutionize the way the Army trains its soldiers."[1]

To turn to a very different situation: " 'Stories are for children,' he said, laughing at my suggestion that we should start the session by reading a children's book," recalls business consultant Diana Hartely:

The people in the room went quiet and lowered their heads, looking tense and embarrassed. This arrogant manager had been provoking me throughout the morning session. I was at a summer school being run by one of world's biggest manufacturers of semi-conductors.

Everyone in the room was at least a director, and the guy who did not want to listen to a story was the company's number five. I took a deep breath, walked forward confidently and placed a chair in front of the class in the way that a schoolteacher sits facing her class. I began to read the story of *Harold and the Purple Crayon* in a sing-song voice, articulating every word and stopping at the bottom of every page to show the picture to my class of leaders. I watched them as I did so, and I began to see that their expressions softened because they were listening to the story not with their intellect but with their inner child. Their inner child, the one who used to believe in the magic of possible worlds, was beginning to come to life; I began to see innocent smiles and looks. Our hero Harold was taking them back to a time in their lives when anything was possible. Even the skeptical executive had calmed down. There was more color in their cheeks, and their faces looked both younger and inspired. It had taken them a few minutes to relax, to believe, like children, that they too could be Harold as he drew his path through the obstacles with thick strokes of fat purple crayon. Now that they had calmed down, the class was ready to accept the idea that change could come about without conflict, personality clashes or tension. These high-level executives were prepared to believe, without any PowerPoint projections, without any graphics and without any pictures, that it simply was possible to play together and to create something that was both innovatory and brilliant.[2]

We have here two types of exercise: military training and a company training session. The stories are not addressed to the same audience and do not have the same objectives. The first is addressed to American troops serving in Iraq, and the second to the executives of a multinational. One trains soldiers to deal with unknown threats in a situation of asymmetrical warfare against terrorism, and the other trains managers to adapt to the unexpected, "the one thing every manager can be certain of in a globalized world." The purpose of the *ES3* video game (*Every Soldier Is a Sensor*) is to trigger rapid and autonomous responses in a hostile environment. In order to do so, it uses the technology of interactive video games. The purpose of leadership training courses is simply to use the magic of narrative to get people to accept "the idea that sudden changes within the company can come about without conflict, personality clashes or tension." The video game teaches troops to repel the enemy; the training course teaches executives to welcome change.

What do command and leadership have in common? What do war and the management of a company have in common? Although they are chosen from sectors that could not be further removed from one another, these two exercises use the same "storytelling" techniques that emerged in the United States in the mid 1990s. They now take increasingly sophisticated forms in both the world of management and that of political communications. They mobilize very different ways of using narrative, from the oral tales told by griots or traditional storytellers to "digital storytelling," which immerse us in multisensory and tightly scripted virtual worlds.

So both managers and military men should tell themselves stories … but to what end? Education and training? But why rely on stories when discipline and expertise previously played that role in, respectively, the army and the world of business? Why should two institutions that are so obedient to the reality principle suddenly begin to obey the rules of efficacious fictions and useful stories? And how long have they been doing so?

The Storytelling Revival

"In recent years, storytelling has been promoted in surprising places," writes the American sociologist Francesca Polletta in her major study of storytelling in politics:

> Managers are now urged to tell stories to motivate workers and doctors are trained to listen to the stories their patients tell. Reporters have rallied around a movement for narrative journalism and psychologists around a movement for narrative therapy. Every year, tens of thousands of people visit the International Storytelling Center in Jonesborough, Tennessee, or flock to one of the more than two hundred storytelling festivals held around the country. And a quick scan of any bookstore reveals scores of popular books on the art of storytelling as a route to spirituality, a strategy for grant seekers, a mode of conflict resolution, and a weight-loss plan.[3]

Long regarded as a form of communication reserved for children and as a marginal leisure activity to be analyzed in literary studies (linguistics, rhetoric, textual grammar, narratology), since the mid 1990s storytelling has enjoyed a surprising success in the United States that has been described as a triumph, a renaissance or a "revival." It is a form of discourse that has come to dominate all sectors of society and that transcends political, cultural, or professional divisions, and it lends credence to the idea of what researchers in the social sciences call the "narrative turn." It has subsequently been likened to the dawn of a new "narrative" age.

But is there really anything new about this? "The essence of American presidential leadership, and the secret of presidential success, is storytelling," writes Evan Cornog, who teaches journalism at Columbia University, in an essay that re-examines the history of American presidencies from George Washington to George W. Bush through the prism of storytelling:

> From the earliest days of the American republic to the present, those seeking the nation's highest office have had to tell persuasive stories — about the nation, about its problems, and, most of all, about themselves — to those who have the power to elect them. Once a president is in office, the ability to tell the right story, and to change the story as necessary, is crucial to the success of his administration. And once a president has left office, he often spends his remaining years working to ensure that the story as he sees it is the one accepted by history. Without a good story, there is no power, and no glory.[4]

Our perception of US history leaves us with a great difficulty distinguishing between true and false, and between what is real and what is fictional. Remember how President Ronald Reagan would sometimes evoke an episode from some old war film as though it were part of the actual history of the United States... That history is cluttered with fictions and legends; witness the often-cited line from John Ford's film *The Man Who Shot Liberty Valance*: "When legend becomes truth, print the legend."

Gilles Deleuze, on the other hand, thought that the superiority of American literature had to do with a certain relationship with the real, with space, and with the idea of the frontier and of conquest. All its great narratives—how the West was won, the legends of the far North, flights to the South—are about crossing borders: "Everything is departure, becoming, passage, leap, daemon, relationship with the outside. They create a new Earth."[5] This narrative construction of the nation was further reinforced by the influx of immigrants throughout the twentieth century. For a long time, America represented much more than a destination on a map and was magnified by Hollywood's images of a "narrative horizon" to which emigrants from all over the world flocked. It was a country where anything was possible. Everyone could write their story on a blank page and start a new life. It was both a nation and a narration.

Many other cultural features testify to the undeniable vitality of the American narrative: the power of the novel from Mark Twain to Don DeLillo, the power of Hollywood movies ever since the studio system was established, the wealth of the folklore transmitted by oral stories and folk songs in the 1950s, the institutionalization of writers' workshops in the universities from the 1960s onwards (which is so alien to the romantic notion of inspiration or the eminently French vision of the lonely, misunderstood genius), or the increase in the number of storytelling festivals, which have mushroomed all over the country ever since the Jonesborough National Storytelling Festival was established in 1972. And yet it would be a mistake to confuse this tradition with the contemporary triumph of storytelling.

In an article entitled "Not The Same Old Story," *Los Angeles Times* staff writer Lynn Smith stresses the novel character of the phenomenon, which transcends disciplinary frontiers and sectors of activity:

From cavemen to scholars, people have been drawn to fire pits, water coolers, theatres and grave sites to share stories ... But since the postmodern literary movement of the 1960s swept out of academia and into the wider culture, narrative thinking has seeped into other fields. Historians, lawyers, physicians, economists and psychologists have all rediscovered the power of stories to frame reality, and storytelling has come to rival logic as a way to understand legal cases, geography, illness or war. Stories have become so pervasive, critics fear they have become a dangerous replacement for facts and reasoned argument ... Persuasive stories can be spun out of false memories or into propaganda. People deceive themselves with their own stories. A story that provides a reassuring explanation of events can also mislead by leaving out contradictions and complexities ... "Before, it was 'That's only a story, give me the facts,' adds Paul Costello, co-founder of the small Center for Narrative Studies in Washington, DC, which was formed six years ago to track the spreading use and practice of narrative. Now, he said, more people are realizing that "stories have real effects that have got to be looked at seriously."[6]

Narrative as Instrument of Control

The success of the narrative approach first became apparent in the field of the human sciences. From about 1995 onwards, this development was described as "the narrativist turn," and it soon spread to the social sciences. In the 1980s, the economist Deirdre N. McCloskey was already defending the idea that economics is essentially a narrative discipline: "It is no accident that the novel and economic science were born at the same time." And the physicist Steven Weinberg was claiming that convincing stories made it possible to channel millions of dollars into research. For his part, Jerome Brunner asserts that "law lives on narrative," while law professor Anthony G. Amsterdam claims that "the narrative presentation of events pervades legal adjudication."[7]

In 2006, a colloquium in Finland made it possible to take stock of the extent of the phenomenon. The theme was "The Traveling Concept of Narrative," and it brought together participants from different disciplines who were interested in the narrative approach. After a centuries-old tradition of travel stories, it is now the very concept of narrative that has begun to drift from one scientific continent to another: from psychology to education, from the social sciences to political science, from medical research to law and theology or the cognitive sciences. In 2000, Brian Richardson observed, "Now, narrative is everywhere." Five years later, James Phelan warned us about the need to be alert to "narrative imperialism."[8]

It is thanks to this shift that storytelling has been able to emerge as a technology of communications, control, and power. The narrativist turn of the mid 1990s in the social sciences coincided with the Internet explosion and the advances in the new information and communications technologies that created the preconditions for the "storytelling revival" and that allowed it to spread so rapidly. NGOs, government agencies, and big companies increasingly discovered the effectiveness of storytelling. In 2006, the American management consultant Lori Silverman noted that NASA, Verizon, Nike, and Land's End all regarded storytelling as the most effective approach to business.[9] Popularized by the highly effective lobbying of new gurus, storytelling management is now regarded as something decision-makers cannot do without, no matter whether they are in politics, economics, telecommunications, the universities, or diplomacy.

If you wish to bring commercial negotiations to a successful conclusion, get rival factions to sign a peace treaty, launch a new product, get a team to accept a major change (including its own firing), design a "serious" video game, or treat GIs suffering from postwar trauma, storytelling is regarded as a panacea. Pedagogues use it as a teaching technique, and psychologists use it as a way of treating traumas. It provides an answer to the crisis of meaning in organizations, and it is a propaganda tool. It is an immersion mechanism, a tool for profiling individuals, a technique for visualizing information, and a powerful way of spreading disinformation.

"I suppose," writes Peter Brooks, a British narratologist who has taught in the United States for a long time, "that literary critics interested in the workings of narrative and the pervasive presence of 'narrativity' in culture ought to be content that their subject of study appears to have colonized large realms of discourse both popular and academic. The problem, however, is that the very promiscuity of the idea of narrative may have rendered the concept useless."[10] The rise of storytelling in fact looks like a Pyrrhic victory and may even have trivialized the very concept of narrative and brought about a deliberate confusion between true narrative and the mere exchange of stories,[11] between eye-witness accounts and fiction, between spontaneous narrativity (oral or written) and annual reports. The instrumental use of narrative for the purposes of management and control has, for instance, resulted in denunciations of the fictional contract (which allows us to distinguish between reality and fiction and to suspend our disbelief for the duration of the story) because it transforms readers into guinea pigs and what management calls "tracked experiences," or, in other words, behaviors that are subject to experimental protocols.

"Stories That Really Tell Us What America Can and Should Be About"

I first heard of the storytelling revival during the winter of 2001. It was March, and I was in the small town of Ithaca, New York. I had been invited by Cornell University to introduce the International Parliament of Writers' "Cities of Asylum" program. After a day of meetings, Anne Berger, who teaches French literature at Cornell and who was the Parliament's US correspondent, invited me to her home for dinner with two friends: Philip Lewis, Professor of French Literature and Dean of Cornell's College of Arts and Sciences, and his wife Catherine Porter, one of the main translators of "French Theory" in the United States. Philip, an amiable bearded man in his fifties, greeted us wearing an apron and took us into the kitchen, where he was finishing preparing dinner, with a big spoon in one hand and the latest issue of the *Chronicle of Higher Education* in the other. The *Chronicle* is the academics' in-house journal and a real institution in academic life. Our host was enthusiastically brandishing the latest issue in a kitchen filled with the aroma of oranges and tarragon. It was like being in a novel by David Lodge.

His enthusiasm was stimulated by an article by Peter Brooks, the academic we have already mentioned. "Stories Abounding" analyzed a recent speech by George W. Bush, who had just been elected to the White House. In it, he used the word "story" no fewer that ten times! Academics are always pleased to discover that their research topic has emerged from their piles of dusty books and been applied to current events. They like nothing so much as noticing that what they were study-ing in solitude has suddenly emerged into the broad light of day.

The article begins by citing the first sentence of Roland Barthes' famous essay "Introduction to the Structural Analysis of Narrative": "The narra-tives of the world are numberless..." The essay gave birth to the new discipline Tzvetan Todorov called "narratology," and which has had con-siderable influence in the United States.[12] Barthes' essay goes on:

> Under this almost infinite diversity of forms, narrative is present in every age, in every place, in every society; it begins with the very history of mankind and there nowhere is or has been a people without narrative. All classes, all human groups, have their narrative, enjoy-ment of which is very often shared by men with very different, even opposing, cultural backgrounds. Caring nothing for the division

between good and bad literature, narrative is international, trans-
historical, transcultural: it is simply there, like life itself.[13]

Peter Brooks comments:

> But Barthes never predicted the coming of a US president who would
> introduce members of his cabinet with the phrase: "Each person has
> got their own story that is so unique: stories really explain what
> America can and should be about." And more simply (in presenting
> Secretary of State Colin Powell), "A great American story." And
> simpler still (in presenting Transportation Secretary Norman Y.
> Mineta), "I love his story." And sure enough, in his brief inaugural
> address, Bush ... starting with "We have a place, all of us, in a long
> story—a story we continue, but whose end we will not see," and
> ending thus: "This story goes on." Again, one has the impression
> that "story" is Bush's embracing category for making sense of the
> world.[14]

We laughed and sat down at the table. It was the autumn of 2001, or
shortly before 9/11, and it was still possible to laugh at George W. Bush
in all innocence. Since then, we have had wars in Afghanistan and Iraq,
Guantánamo and Abu Ghraib, and jokes about Bush Jr. no longer have
the same flavor.

How could Roland Barthes' idea that narrative is one of the great categories of knowledge that we use to understand and organize the world
come to dominate political subculture, management methods, and advertising? What are we to think of the new vulgate that tells us that all
discourses—political, ideological, or cultural—should adopt a narrative
form? By way of explanation, Brooks stressed that TV series were
having a growing impact on the lives of Americans, and even on his academic colleagues. He cited the example of friends who would rather
watch *The West Wing* than CNN news. According to Brooks, both political communications and journalism "overused" the notion of narrative.

Two months later, *Loft Story* triumphed on French television. *Big
Brother* was already a hit in most European countries.[15] And after 9/11,
the United States succumbed to a narrative fever that was to find expression in everything from the archaic form of oral stories and folk songs
to the technologies of digital storytelling (webcams, blogs, interactive

television). In the reality TV studios, as on video game consoles, the screens of mobile phones and computers, and from bedrooms to cars, reality is now caught in a narrative net that filters perceptions and stimulates useful emotions.

The great narratives that punctuate human history—from Homer to Tolstoy and from Sophocles to Shakespeare—told of universal myths and transmitted the lessons learned by past generations. They passed on lessons in wisdom that were the fruit of cumulative experience. Storytelling goes in the opposite direction: it tacks artificial narratives on to reality, blocks exchanges, and saturates symbolic space with its series and stories. It does not talk about past experience. It shapes behaviors and channels flows of emotion. Far from being the "course of recognition" that Paul Ricoeur detected in narrative activity,[16] storytelling establishes narrative systems that lead individuals to identify with models and to conform to protocols.

A Worrying Proliferation

The aim of this book is to retrace this history by analyzing the unprecedented development of this instrumental use of narrative. Where did it begin? How are we to explain its rise in the United States and then in Europe, and in activities that were previously governed by rational argument or scientific discourse? Who are the agents of its production? What is at stake in its symbolic construction, and what are its figures? What obscure paths have allowed it to spread from the central apparatuses of power to the most individual practices? Is it a top-down process, or does it obey a logic of contagion that allows it to spread from one sector to another? To what extent is it legitimized by the narrative approach in the social sciences? What role does technology or ideology play in its proliferation?

Thanks to the Internet, we now enjoy an abundance of information that was inaccessible ten years ago. In the time it took to write this book, the number of times the word "storytelling" turned up on the Internet increased threefold. It is being used more often by the day and has moved from institutional sites (companies, consultants, universities) to the main American newspapers, and to the webzines and blogs that constitute new spaces from which it can spread still further. These observations are not purely methodological—it was the Web that allowed me to conduct my survey by taking a critical look at the incredible diversity of its documentary resources. They are an integral part of the phenomenon we are studying, which would be unthinkable without the incessant noise of its statements and discourses.

I examine these new uses of narrative in seven chapters that are so many stages in a journey through the virtual world of storytelling, with its writing machines, its tracking and control systems, its narrative spirals, its formats and its networks. In order to do so, I studied the emotion-producing industries that give us collective fables. They include, of course, Hollywood and Disney, but also Nike, Coca-Cola, Adobe, and Microsoft, Xerox's factories and the glass towers of the World Bank, which is where the first experiment in storytelling management was carried out. I have also had to decipher the discourse of the management gurus and griots, which stimulate useful affects and spread, thanks to their performativity, the "stories of the heroes and heroines who make success possible."[17] I have analyzed the websites of the media consultancies who sell the dream society in which work will be directed by stories and emotions, and in which we will buy not just commodities but also the stories they tell. And I have explored the other side of the dream society, the "non-fictional" reality of the sweatshops of Latin America where the labor of children is exploited, and the Indian call centers where young recruits learn to "become American" by watching TV series. I have also looked at the activities of the White House's spin doctors, who claim to be able to use storytelling to create political realities that are always new, and at the aforementioned Institute for Creative Technologies in Los Angeles.

The first chapter deals with marketing. It describes how the technologies that make it possible to sell commodities were, over a period of some fifteen years, displaced from product to logo, and then from logo to story. The brand image that dominated marketing in the 1980s was replaced by the "brand story" from 1995 onwards. This change implies the appearance of a new lexicon in which "audience" replaces "consumers" and "narrative sequences" replace advertising "campaigns."

Chapter 2 traces the invention of storytelling management in the 1990s, charged with using shared narrative to mobilize emotions. This discourse is addressed primarily to managers; its function is to transform the virtues of autonomy and responsibility, leadership and innovation, and flexibility and adaptability into narratives.

Chapter 3 identifies the three constituent elements of the neo-management of the first decade of the twenty-first century: 1) the injunction to change; 2) the management of emotions, which goes hand in hand with the constitution of capitalism's new "subject"—a consumer, wage-earner or manager—who is defined as a "suffering self" and an emotional self; 3) the use of stories to manage that emotional ego.

Chapter 4 looks at the link between these new mobilizing techniques and the appearance of a new form of labor organization that is mutant, centralized, and nomadic. Its ideal is adaptation to a changing and unpredictable environment, and the adaptation of the quest for profit to ever shorter cycles.

Chapter 5 is devoted to storytelling's hold over political discourses in the United States. It evokes the trauma of Watergate, the executive's obsessions with controlling the media, and the invention of spin doctors under Ronald Reagan and of story spinners under Clinton. It also looks at how, under George W. Bush, Karl Rove's "Scheherazade strategy" made storytelling the key to winning and exercising power.

Chapter 6 analyzes the growing convergence between the Pentagon and Hollywood, which led to the establishment of the Institute for Creative Technologies in 1999. This was a production studio that brought together army experts and Hollywood's best scriptwriters. Within five years it became the main producer of video games designed to recruit and train military personnel.

Chapter 7 reveals, finally, how, from September 11, 2001 onwards, American diplomacy adopted a marketing logic, even going so far as to recruit "branding" specialists for diplomatic positions, whose job is to "sell America to the world as a brand."

The art of narrative—which, ever since it emerged, has recounted humanity's experience by shedding light on it—has become, like storytelling, an instrument that allows the state to lie and to control public opinion. Behind the brands and the TV series, and in the shadows of victorious election campaigns from Bush to Sarkozy, as well as in those of military campaigns in Iraq and elsewhere, there are dedicated storytelling technicians. The empire has confiscated narrative. This book tells the incredible story of how it has hijacked the imaginary.

1   From Logo to Story

In 2000, Canadian journalist Naomi Klein wrote in her book *No Logo*: "The astronomical growth in the wealth and cultural influence of multinational corporations over the last fifteen years can arguably be traced back to a single, seemingly innocuous idea developed by management theorists in the mid-1980s: that successful corporations must primarily produce brands, as opposed to products."[1] Ten years later, the same theorists had changed their minds; corporations must produce stories, as opposed to brands.

According to Seth Godin, an American innovator in viral marketing, the new marketing is "about telling stories, not selling commercials."[2] And according to Laurence Vincent, the author of *Legendary Brands*, "Legendary brands are based on narrative construction, and the narrative they tell is the basis of their empathetic consumer affinity."[3] For his part, William Ryan, the man who transformed Apple's image when the iMac was launched, asserts that we should "Forget traditional positioning and brand-centric approaches. We're now in the 'Age of the Narrative' where the biggest challenge facing companies is how to tell their story in the most compelling, consistent, and credible way possible — both internally and externally."[4]

So what happened in the space of ten years? Why does marketing now recommend the brand story rather than the brand image? Have logos lost their aura? How can we explain why the companies we described as postmodern or postindustrial suddenly abandoned the path of branding, which made them so successful in the 1990s, and began to explore the uncharted realm of pre-modern myths and fabulous stories?

The aura of a brand used to come from the product; people who liked the Ford brand drove Ford cars all their lives. Singer owed its prestige to the sewing machine, which was both a piece of furniture and a tool that was handed down from one generation to the next. "By the end of the 1940s," Naomi Klein writes, "there was a burgeoning awareness that a brand wasn't just a mascot or a catchphrase or a picture painted on the label of a company's product; the company as a whole could have a brand identity or a "corporate consciousness," as this ephemeral quality was termed at the time."[5] By the beginning of the 1980s, General Motors' advertisements were already telling "stories about the people who drove its cars—the preacher, the pharmacist or the country doctor who, thanks to his trusty GM, arrives 'at the bedside of a dying child' just in time 'to bring it back to life.' "[6] But the advertising still focused on the product, its uses and its qualities, whereas companies like Nike, Microsoft, and, later, Tommy Hilfiger and Intel were already turning away from products and producing brand-images rather than objects.

Brands in Crisis

Nothing, apparently, had changed at the beginning of the new millennium: the number of brands registered in the United States was constantly increasing (140,000 new trade marks in 2003—100,000 more than in 1983). Big companies were still spending billions of dollars on sponsorship,[7] and David Foster Wallace's joke in his novel *Infinite Jest* about an America in which corporations would sponsor entire years— the Year of the Whopper, the Year of the Depend Adult Undergarment[8]—no longer seemed far-fetched.

"In the past decade, corporations looking to navigate an ever more competitive marketplace have embraced the gospel of branding with newfound fervor," wrote James Surowiecki in a demystifying article on "The Decline of Brands" in November 2004:

> The brand value of companies like Coca-Cola and IBM is routinely calculated at tens of billions of dollars, and brands had come to be seen as the ultimate long-term asset—economic agents capable of withstanding turbulence and generating profits for decades ... Even as companies have spent enormous amounts of time and energy introducing new brands and defending established ones, Americans have become less loyal.[9]

According to the retail-tracking firm NPD Group, nearly half those who described themselves as highly loyal to a brand were no longer loyal a year later. Because consumers were more promiscuous, established brands were vulnerable, and new ones had a real chance of succeeding. One index of this vulnerability was that the brands that had been the symbol of the multinationals' prosperity in the 1990s had suddenly lost their prestige and commercial power. Nokia, the brand ranked sixth in the world in 2002, saw its sales collapse the following year and suffered a loss of $6 billion. Krispy Kreme, described as "hottest brand" by *Fortune* magazine in 2003, and with an estimated value of $30 billion, was dethroned by Atkins in 2004.[10] "Paradoxical," "incomprehensible" and "unpredictable" were the words that marketers have used most often to describe consumer behavior since the beginning of the millennium. "Just ten years ago," according to the September 18, 2006, issue of the French business paper *Les Echos*, "socioprofessional categories were enough to identify consumers" habits and even their desires. Alas. The way our modern societies are developing demonstrates the obsolescence of that approach by the day."[11] At the same time, the director of studies for the opinion-polling firm IPSOS stated: "We are addressing consumers who are no longer under the brands' spell; they have become experts ... and that makes them difficult to handle."[12] For his part, Rémy Sansaloni, head of market research and documentation at TNS/Média Intelligence and author of a book entitled *The Neo-consumer: How Consumers Are Regaining their Power*, took the view that "Consumers are reacting to the anarchic development of pseudo-innovations, promotions right, left and center, and the way mass marketing is standardizing supply, by making themselves scarce."[13]

The birth of new media, and the huge opportunities for "viral" advertising opened up by the Internet, have put an end to the unchallenged power of advertising and television. The era of brand advertising is coming to an end. More and more death notices are being posted. According to the authors of the bestselling *The Fall of Advertising*, "Advertising has lost its power ... Advertising has no credit with consumers, who are increasingly sceptical of its claims."[14] And according to former Coca-Cola marketing director Sergio Zyman, writing in 2002, "Advertising, as you know it, is dead ... It doesn't work, it's a colossal waste of money, and if you don't wise up it could end up destroying ... your brand."[15]

Beneath the Swoosh, the Sweatshops

"At the beginning of October 2003, the population of Vienna was intrigued to find that a strange container had taken up residence in one of the city's main squares," the Geneva-based newspaper *Le Courrier* reported on October 31, 2003. The container, which bore the legend "Nikeground. Rethinking Space," informed the population that the square had been bought by Nike, and that it was therefore going to be renamed "Nikeplatz." A red swoosh—the stylized comma used as a logo by the sports gear firm—measuring 18 meters by 36—would be flown over Vienna. "Hostesses, all dressed in Nike, explained to visitors that the legendary brand would be present all over Europe: over the next few years, Nikesquares, Nikestreets, Piazzanikes and Nikestraßes would flourish in all the great capitals of the world."

Nike was forced to react. "This operation is a fraud; we have nothing to do with it. It is a violation of copyright," explained a spokesperson for the company. It was soon discovered that a mischievous artists' collective with the unlikely name of 0100101110101101.org was behind the operation. It explained on its website that its goal was to "produce a collective hallucination that could change the way the Viennese saw their city." Nike's ire provoked some amused reactions from the impish artists, reported *Le Courrier*: "'Where is the famous Nike spirit? I expected to be dealing with sportspeople and not a bunch of boring lawyers,' explained a spokesman for the collective."[16]

Nike lodged a complaint and, in a thirty-page document sent to the Austrian Ministry of Justice, demanded the immediate removal of the installations—real and virtual—in the name of brand protection. One is reminded of Naomi Klein's ironic comment: "Branding ... is a balloon economy: it inflates with astonishing rapidity but it is full of hot air. It shouldn't be surprising that this formula has bred armies of pin-wielding critics, eager to burst the corporate balloon."[17]

By the end of the 1990s, anti-brand movements were spreading rapidly. Groups of activists and artists like the "Reclaim the Streets" movement began to challenge the way the brands were taking over public space. The "labeling" of all human activity (commercial and otherwise, economic and cultural), the way humanitarian NGOs and ecological struggles were being commercialized by branding, and the logos' tyranny over the whole of social life, were met with a wave of increasingly virulent protests. This was a paradoxical phenomenon: the more a brand identified with transgressive value, the more protests it generated. That is what happened to Nike.

From 1995 onwards, in light of many studies carried out in Asia, Africa, and Latin America, public opinion in the industrialized countries began to learn about the working conditions of the men and women who make the divine garments and the flying sneakers. "In China, the vast majority of women workers are paid much less than the legal minimum wage," the Berne Declaration (a Swiss NGO campaigning for fair trade) stated in 2002. "On average, they work twelve hours a day and up to seven days a week, in violation of both Chinese legislation and Nike's code. The situation is similar in Vietnam and Indonesia."[18]

Growing numbers of NGO campaigns in the United States, Canada, Australia, and Europe described working conditions in these sweatshops. In California, Nike was taken to court and charged with misleading advertising. Michael Moore's film *The Big One*, in which Nike's Chairman and CEO Phillip Knight justifies the child labor of fourteen-year-olds, had a devastating effect on the swoosh brand. Speaking in Brussels at a conference on the growing power of anti-corporate groups, Peter Verhille of the PR firm Entente International admitted that "one of the major strengths of the pressure groups … is their ability to exploit the instruments of the telecommunications revolution. Their agile use of global tools such as the Internet reduces the advantage that corporate budgets once provided."[19]

The anti-Nike movement's campaigns were revealing globalization's black holes: they shed light on the invisible links between the brands and their sub-contractors, between the marketing agencies and the underground workshops, between the footballs used by the athletes at the 2008 World Cup and the hands of the children who made them. Beneath Nike's swoosh, the sweatshops. On May 12, 1998, Phillip Knight told a press conference at the National Press Club in Washington that the company was taking initiatives "to further improve factory working conditions worldwide and provide increased opportunities for people who manufacture Nike products," and admitted that Nike had become "synonymous with slave wages, forced overtime, and arbitrary abuse."[20]

These measures could, at best, put an end to the scandal of the sweatshops. Was Nike about to commit itself to a new labor policy? But would that be enough to restore the brand's magic, or at least to appear to do so? The reason why demonstrations and artistic performances had succeeded in undermining Nike's swoosh was that the image was no longer enough. The brand had to be based upon something less volatile than a slogan, an elegant logo, or an eye-catching commercial.

What's in a Name?

Theorists of branding were summoned to the brand's bedside. MTV's founder Tom Freston had already issued a warning in 1998: "You can beat a brand to death."[21] Everyone was agreed about one thing: brands were sick. Serious questions were being asked about their future: "It can take 100 years to build up a good brand and 30 days to knock it down," complained John Hancock Mutual Life Insurance president in January 1999.[22] Branding evangelist Tom Peters wondered: "How much is enough? Nobody knows for sure. It's pure art. Leverage is good. Too much leverage is bad."[23] Kevin Roberts, CEO of the Saatchi and Saatchi advertising agency and author of *Lovemarks* agreed: "Brands have run out of juice. They're dead."[24]

Nike was a victim of its own excessive fame, and Wall Street commented that it had "outswooshed itself."[25] So can a brand's fame plateau, and then begin to depreciate and lose its influence? According to James Surowiecki, brands do indeed wear out: "They're becoming nothing more than shadows. You wouldn't expect your shadow to protect you or show you the way."[26] The firms decided to go back to basics. The role of marketing is to sell, and that objective can be obtained in various different ways: through aggressive advertising or material inducements, directly or indirectly with advertisements that have a subliminal influence, but also by involving the consumer in a long-term emotional relationship. That is the brand's role: to "involve" the consumer. That is why brands are effective, and why they are mysterious.

In the famous passage on commodity fetishism in *Capital*, Marx writes: "If commodities could speak, they would say this: our use-value may interest men, but it does not belong to us as objects. What does belong to us as objects, however, is our value."[27] What was for Marx no more than a rhetorical hypothesis has become a reality: brands have begun to speak. And "when these brands speak, consumers listen intently. When these brands act, consumers follow ... These brands are not just marketing constructs: they are figures in the consumer's life."[28]

In the 1990s, brands began to express themselves through dazzling logos — Apple's apple, Nike's swoosh, the oil company's shell, McDonald's golden arches — and all kinds of pictograms. The product was dissolved into the brand. Within a decade, the logo, even more so than money, had become the sign of wealth. And the brand became a pure value that shimmered in the sky of the stock exchanges. James Suroweicki made the point that

> Marketers aren't completely deceived (or being deceiving) when they argue that consumers make emotional bonds with brands, but those connections are increasingly tenuous … Gurus talk about building an image to create a halo over a company's products. But these days, the only sure way to keep a brand strong is to keep on wheeling out new products, which will in turn cast the halo. (The iPod has made a lot more people interested in Apple than Apple made people interested in the iPod).[29]

"What's in a name?" asked Shakespeare in *Romeo and Juliet*. "That which we call a rose/By any other name would smell as sweet." Ashraf Ramzy — a marketing consultant whose clients include Nissan, Canon, and KLM — and Alicia Korten asked the same question of brands in 2006.[30] What's in a brand? An image? A reputation? What is the unique and indefinable thing that defines a company for its clients and that makes it different from its competitors? Is there such a thing as a brand essence? Or does its aura develop from familiarity with the brand and its market because we have seen the advertising campaigns or seen the product on the supermarket shelves? Does it emerge from ferocious battles with its competitors? Some saw brands as images that were as abstract and eternal as possible. They were signs or signifiers, not signifieds. Others put the emphasis on their historical nature.

In the almost metaphysical debates that were born of the realization that the prescriptive power of brands had been exhausted, the latter view prevailed and cleverly exploited the wave of protests about the social realities that lay behind the logos. Luc Boltanski and Eve Chiapello have clearly demonstrated that the "spirit of capitalism" renews itself by integrating its opponents' criticisms: "To maintain its powers of attraction, capitalism therefore has to draw upon resources external to itself, beliefs which, at a given moment in time, possess considerable powers of persuasion."[31] The vocabulary and spirit of the management of the 1990s were, for example, imbued with the demands of May '68's students as they protested against what they saw as an over-materialist society, with the movement's values (imagination, autonomy, authenticity), and even some of its slogans, such as the premonitory and over-familiar "Object, hide yourself," or the question which, thirty years after the event, had become a marketing cliché: "Are you consumers or participants?"

By the end of the 1990s, Nike no longer made anyone dream. Its name, slogan, and products had become bogged down in a shameful narrative that demonized its divine brand. No-logo activists had unexpected answers to the questions the marketing people were asking themselves: beneath the smooth logos of the brands one could see the women workers in Indonesia who assembled Nike's sneakers, the child-slaves of Honduras who made sports gear for the Wal-Mart distribution chain, or the young women in Haiti who made "Pocahontas" pajamas for Disney, who were so exhausted that they had to feed their babies sugared water. Stories of suffering and exploitation. In June 1996, *Life* magazine published photographs of Pakistani children making footballs bearing Nike's logo. The pictures were seen all over the world. Brands concealed stories, and they were ugly stories. If those stories were to be done away with, and if the brands had to be saved, edifying stories had to be made up as a matter of urgency. And what better way to do that than to call on the services of the protesters?

In August 1999, Amanda Tucker, the director of the ILO's anti-child-labor program, was recruited by Nike. At the same time, Nike commissioned a report from some American academics. Throughout the 1990s, David M. Boje, who was one of the pioneers of "organizational story-telling," had been involved in anti-Nike campaigns and, together with his students, had done theoretical work that deconstructed the Nike brand. According to Boje, companies were storytelling organizations. They were sites for multiple narratives and for a dialogue between stories that either contradicted or complemented one another. They were undermined from within by issues that were narrative as well as economic, financial, or industrial. David Boje took his inspiration from Roland Barthes' narratology as well as Guy Debord's thesis on the society of the spectacle; he also referred to the Russian semiologist Mikhail Bakhtin's theories about the dialogic or polyphonic nature of narrative. Using all these inputs, Boje developed the paradigm for a new postmodern organization that would constantly mutate and would communicate both internally and externally thanks to alternating strategies of narration and counter-narration.

The exploitation stories that had demystified the Nike brand had to be challenged by other narratives or counter-narratives. The brand was no longer self-sufficient and had to become a vector for stories. If it reformulated its labor policy and made certain ecological commitments, explained Boje, Nike could create a new identity for itself "just in time." Nike was not in the process of improving its moral standing, but just changing its story.[32]

The Brand Is a Story

From the beginning of the millennium onwards, those who ran the big American corporations therefore embarked upon ambitious projects to reconstruct their brands as narratives. The branding theorists who advised them converted to storytelling. Ashraf Ramzy, for instance, defines himself as a "mythmaker." In 2002, he opened a strategy consultancy in Amsterdam and called it 'Narrativity Strategy & Story B.V.' His credo is: "People do not buy products; they buy the stories those products represent. Nor do they buy brands; they buy into the myths and archetypes these brands symbolize."[33] He gives several examples, including whisky producer Chivas Brothers. By the late 1990s, the brand had begun to lose its prestige. Chivas Regal's international marketing manager, Han Zantingh, explained: "Chivas was a whisky your father drank, something you gave as a gift but wouldn't drink yourself. The brand was known but completely not relevant ... We wanted to support and nourish our brand essence: rich and generous. The original Chivas Brothers ultimately made a rich and generous blend because they themselves had a rich and generous attitude [towards] life."[34] The best way to nourish the brand was to use a good story. Chivas' marketers therefore decided to re-write its history. A journalist was hired to tell the story of its glory days. The result was "The Chivas Legend," which consists of twelve episodes from the centuries-old story of a twelve-year-old whisky.

The story begins when Chivas was granted a royal warrant by the Queen during a visit to Balmoral in the nineteenth century. Chivas Brothers became royal suppliers to the throne. It continues with the story of the first malt, produced by the oldest distilleries in the High-lands: they were built in 1786. Then we reach the 1950s, when the brand's success in the United States resonated with the spirit of the times—Dean Martin, Sammy Davis Jr., and Frank Sinatra. All these 'richly evocative' stories merge into one: The Chivas Legend, which now circulates in bars and discotheques, passed on by storytellers, just as stories were passed on in the good old days. They are now called "brand ambassadors." Zantingh concludes: "By creating *The Chivas Legend*, we reconnected our heritage and our audience. It not only stopped the decline of our market share in a brutally competitive arena, it reversed the trend. Our sales volume is now growing at double-digit rates."[35]

According to storytelling management's guru Steve Denning, "A brand is essentially a relationship."[36] This relationship may be tenuous and fragile, and may mean simply that the consumer is vaguely familiar with the brand name, or it may be long term. The paradox of modern marketing is in fact that it must develop consumer loyalty at a time when buying behaviors have become changeable, labile, and unpredictable. It has to bring fickle consumers back to the fold of the brand, and encourage them to commit themselves to a long-term emotional rela-tionship. "Say it with stories," suggests Brand Advocate, a "relational marketing agency" that makes "three-minute minifilms" telling stories featuring the target clients. "No one has ever denied the power of stories," asserted the French business magazine *L'Entreprise* when it reported this experiment.[37]

For today's marketers, making a brand famous or familiar to a mass of anonymous consumers is no longer enough; they have to create a unique emotional relationship between a brand and those who are loyal to it. This is relational marketing. "The job of a marketer today is to aggregate people. It's not about eyeballs. It's about engagement," states Larry Weber, a marketing consultant who specializes in the new media.[38] For that to happen, the brand must rediscover a strong and coherent identity that speaks to consumers as well as to the company's collaborators— employees, shareholders, suppliers, investors—and condense all the elements that go to make up the company into a coherent story: its history, the nature of the products its makes, the quality of its customer-care, labor relations, and its relationship with the environment.

According to Ashraf Ramzy, Levi Strauss Signature's CEO Scott Laporta took up this challenge when he had to relaunch a brand that was losing its target customers: "We were a company that sold riveted jeans to gold miners. Yet our company was no longer targeting working-class heroes," explained Laporta.[39] How could anyone sell a brand to the working class, when Levi Strauss was not present in discount chains like Wal-Mart or Target? Levi Strauss's marketers went out to collect stories from the chains' customers.

A young woman called Heidi, who lived in a tract house in Pueblo, Colorado, told them that she was willing to drive sixty miles to buy a brand, not for herself (she did not wear Levis) but for her kids. Marketing director Michael Perman asked her why these brands were so important to her. She said that "the stuff at Wal-Mart" was "for other people," meaning "the people on welfare," the poor, the unemployed, and retired people. "What a profound moment for us. She wanted a brand that respected her. This had value. She was willing to go sixty miles for this. She thought the retail representation [in the value channel] was disrespectful to her. What a profound opportunity if we could provide her with something that would bring her respect." "The story of a working-class woman named Heidi brought the company back to its roots and inspired the creation and launch of the Levi Strauss Signature brand," explained Laporta.[40]

The example of Levi Strauss shows that storytelling is not just an effective way of attracting consumers and winning their loyalty. Marketers use this tool to understand what consumers think of the brand. *Les Echos* journalist Sophie Peters remarked in September 2006 that "traditional surveys have reached their limits." Tired of being asked about anything and everything, and of endless questionnaires, the people being surveyed were reluctant to answer the interviewers' questions, even when they were paid to do so. The marketers' new weapon is "consumer insight." This new approach has become standard for those industrialists who install cameras in private homes or who are so "bold as to send their workers to interview consumers in their own homes." Neuromarketing goes still further; it uses the new techniques of medical imaging to observe consumers' brain activity and subjects them to different stimuli or narrative schemata. Michel Reynard notes that at TNS Sofres, observation has been developed to the point of paranoia.[41]

The "Narrative World" of Brands

In less than fifteen years, marketing has moved from products to logos, and then from logos to stories, from brand image to brand story. So much so that the title of Naomi Klein's fine book, which had become synonymous with resistance to the tyranny of brands, could now be seen as neomarketing's injunction: *"No logo: stories."*

It is not as though commodities and brands have disappeared. They are still there, as present as ever, but they have lost their status as objects or "reified" images. They talk to us and captivate us by telling us stories that fit in with our expectations and worldviews. When they are used on the Web, they transform us into storytellers. We spread their stories. Good stories are so fascinating that we are encouraged to tell them again.

Barbara B. Stern, a professor in Rutgers University's Department of Marketing, has shown that literary forms such as the ballad, the epic, metaphor, and irony have a growing influence on marketing. "What branding really is, is a story attached to a product. When you have a product that's just like another product, there are any number of ways to compete. The stupid way is to lower prices. The smart way is to change the value of the product by telling a story about it."[42]

It has become a commonplace to speak of the fragmentation of values, the loss of points of reference and the shattering of codes of behavior: consumers are no longer attracted to products, or even lifestyles, but they are attracted to "narrative worlds." In times of economic crisis, when nostalgia marketing invokes the recurrent memory of some golden age, it mobilizes worlds that rely heavily on narratives. One brand of furniture, for instance, markets its "Bogart Collection" to celebrate "the return to all the style and elegance of Hollywood's most romantic age," while its Ernest Hemingway Collection is supposedly the embodiment of the "reputation and respect" inspired by the author and "his" line of furniture.[43]

Given this proliferation of signs, neomarketing explains, consumers are looking for stories that allow them to reconstruct coherent worlds. It is now estimated that consumers in the industrialized countries are exposed to some 3,000 commercials every day. Brands that do not want to be swamped by this tide of advertising have to make themselves stand out, as Christian Budtz explains in his *Storytelling: Branding in Practice*: "Does your company have an original story to tell? A story that is so honest, captivating and unique, that we are willing to pay a price premium to become part of it? Brands must build on an honest, authentic story that appeals to consumers' personal values."[44]

Not everyone endorses this naïve justification for the recourse to stories. As the title of Seth Godin's book puts it so cynically: "all marketers are liars." He contends that "marketers lie to consumers because consumers demand it. Marketers tell the stories, and consumers believe them."[45] He goes on:

> There are new mothers who believe that happiness lies in the next new educational product for their infant, and there are bodybuilders who believe that the next nutritional supplement will provide them with the shortcut to a perfect body. There are environmentalists who are certain that the next scientific innovation will be mankind's last, and xenophobes who know for sure that black helicopters from the United Nations are due to arrive tomorrow. Each of these groups wants to hear stories that support its worldview. Each group ... sees itself as near the center, not on the fringe, and each group very much wants to be catered for.[46]

Disney, for example, came up with the idea of marketing educational videos entitled *Baby Einstein*. They were designed to stimulate the cognitive abilities of newborns and were supposed to give them a competitive edge over other babies or even transform them into "little Einsteins." The videos, which are produced by a division of Disney, were wildly successful and made $14 million for the company, even though they were "virtually useless." The explanation is simple: they were aimed not so much at infants as at their mothers and were in keeping with the legitimate intellectual ambitions they had for their children. By buying these "educational videos," they were buying a "success story" for their newborn babies and were thus complicit in the company's storytelling: "Stories let us lie to ourselves. And those lies satisfy our ideas. It's the story, not the good or the service you actually sell, that pleases the consumer."[47] Godin also gives the example of ethical investment, "which won't appeal to everyone."[48] But by merging two apparently contradictory ideas, it is possible to create a story to which many consumers will listen. The Acumen Fund envisions an organization that will take the best of the nonprofit world and blend it with the best elements of capitalism ... They are choosing to tell a story to those *dissatisfied* with the traditional stories charities would like them to believe. They are reaching entrepreneurs looking for a different, more efficient philanthropic alternative, as well as foundations that are eager to make a name for themselves by funding organizations with a non-traditional approach to philanthropy.

As Godin remarks with glee, all sorts of oxymorons now become possible: Non-donation Philanthropy. Return-on-Philanthropy. Social Capital Dividends.[49] "The words and images you use to tell a story are powerful tools. When those words or images conflict, you've created an oxymoron. Jumbo shrimp and military intelligence are the clichés, but there are countless success stories that were built around oxymorons."[50] They make it possible to reach groups of consumers who are often overlooked. There are more and more of them, and they are trying to reconcile contradictory desires. That is a good definition of "buyer's neurosis," which may be triggered by Starbucks' soy-based decaf or "adventure cruises" in Lapland. Oxymorons destabilize our incredulity or skepticism reflexes and have a surprise effect that intrigues, seduces, and captivates us. This is what every narrative theorist since Coleridge calls "the temporary suspension of disbelief."

More generally, marketers are being invited to reform their vocabulary. According to Laurence Vincent, they must abandon the lexicon of traditional marketing and becomes storytellers. They must stop thinking in terms of "strategic plans" and see brands as stories, and "advertising campaigns" as "narrative sequences": "Instead of strategic plans, they need to think of their brand myth or narrative. Instead of consumers, they need to think of audiences. Instead of spokespeople, sponsors, and products, they need to think of characters in a larger story. Instead of retail environments, they need to think of narrative settings."[51]

The Dream Society

The ambitions of twenty-first-century marketing do not, however, stop at the supermarket door: they extend to the world itself. Its ambition is no longer simply to promote the benefits of the consumer society; it seeks to "produce" a new society and a new world. It makes no secret of its messianic nature: "Hundreds of thousands of Sudanese have died because of bad marketing. Religions thrive or fade away because of the marketing choices they make."[52] For Seth Godin, it is very simple: "If marketers could tell a better story—taking your medicine or sending peacekeepers where they are needed—we would all benefit."[53]

The Danish futurologist Ralph Jensen, director of the Copenhagen Institute for Future Studies and author of *The Dream Society*, looks even further into the future. In 2001, he founded Dream Company Ltd and runs its "Imagination" division.[54] Its mission is to persuade most of the companies in the world that we are making the transition from one society to another. Between now and 2020, the next major stage in the development of society will, he argues, be the "dream era." In the "dream society," all products will tell consumers a story: "*The Dream Society* traces the way in which a consumer culture like ours tells stories through the products we buy: clothes, transportation, leisure-products, vacations, homes. In the dream society, our work will be driven by stories and emotions." For his part, the French designer Philippe Starck is no longer satisfied with furnishing interiors with objects; he wants to give "more happiness": "Within ten years, the functional objects in our home will be replaced by non-material services. When that happens, our home will be full of nothing but sentimental things."[55]

The idea that being invaded by sentimental things is not necessarily an attractive prospect, especially if those sentimental things are reified forms of the consumer society, is endorsed by the analysis of Georges Lewi, who teaches at the Haute Ecole de Commerce top business school and who, in 1998, justified the way our contemporaries have become trapped in the mythical world of the commodity in these terms: "Today's consumers need to believe in their brands in the same way that the Greeks believed in their myths."[56] Establishing a parallel between brands and myths, he argues that the mechanisms governing the Microsoft saga are the same as those behind the Apollo myth. The Intel myth is a sort of Dionysian miracle, while Bouygues apparently has something in common with Hephaestus. From this perspective, brands become myths when they begin to resonate with consumers' beliefs. According to Lewi, there are three stages in the life cycle of a brand: a heroic period in which it stands out because it is different; a phase of wisdom, when it becomes confident; and a mythical phase in which it acquires consciousness. "The resurgence of myths within our contemporary society," claims

Lewi, "is particularly obvious in periods of globalized insecurity, which stimulate our need to seek out the truth and the meaning of life, as well as our thirst for magic and mystery." Witness the commercial success of the books of J. R. R. Tolkien and J. K. Rowling in the West: "They are in fact stories and tales that draw on our heritage of fairy tales and that speak to our globalized imaginary and at the same time give us a feeling of belonging."

This feeling of belonging involves, however, a certain "mind-formatting," as Scott Rosenberg explained in an article in the webzine *Salon* in 1998. Storytelling is, he wrote, "The apotheosis of the ideology of marketing. … It transfers promotional thinking from the company level to the personal level, forcing the most private relationships and transactions into a template shaped by the business world."[57] For Tom Peters, the author of the famous 1997 article "The Brand Called You," this development was inevitable.[58] He argues that we are being called upon to be our own consumers. American Express's campaign slogan, "My life, my card," for instance, associates the use of the credit card with memorable episodes in our lives to such an extent that using the card becomes one such episode.

The goal of storytelling marketing is not just to persuade consumers to buy a product but to plunge them into a narrative world, to involve them in a credible story. It is no longer a matter of seducing or convincing consumers; the point is to produce a belief-effect. The goal is no longer to stimulate demand, but to offer a life-story that provides certain integrated behavioral models. The act of buying something actually becomes part of the narrative. No matter whether you are young or old, unemployed or working, in good health or ill with cancer, "you are the story" and you are its hero. Neomarketing brings about a subtle semantic shift: it transforms consumption into amateur dramatics. Pick a part, and we will supply the stage set and the costumes.

Consumption becomes the only way of relating to the world. Brands are given the powers we once sought in myths or drugs: break on through to the other side, experience a weightless self, get high, take a trip; it used to be Icarus or LSD, and now it is Nike or Adidas. Sneakers defy the law of gravity. Skiing, surfing, and skating give us access to the supernatural. "Nike president cum sneaker shaman" Tom Clarke explains that "the inspiration of sports allows us to rebirth ourselves constantly."[59]

Brands are vectors for "worlds": they lead us into a fictional story, a world that has been scripted and developed by "experimental marketing" agencies whose ambition is no longer to meet or even to create needs, but to make "worldviews" converge.

The use of universal Jungian archetypes in international marketing should, in theory, allow the same marketing strategies to be used all over the world. To take one striking example: according to a study carried out in 2003 by Booz Allen, 9/11 did not change the way American brands such as Nike, Kraft, Motorola, Exxon-Mobil, Ford, Coca-Cola, or Pepsi are perceived in Muslim countries.[60] Quite the contrary. There is more hostility towards American brands in the United Kingdom or China than in Muslim countries. According to the authors, the explanation for this surprising finding is that the narrative of an American global brand is "understood foremost as global, not American." The other reason is that, ever since the 1990s, multinationals have been making an effort to understand "the local narrative" and to integrate the narrative codes of Muslim countries into their global narratives.

Storytelling marketing is, by its own admission, an attempt to synchronize "worldviews" that may well be antagonistic in political or religious terms, but which can be reconciled on the great stage of the world market. The exercise of consuming then becomes an exercise in global communications or even communion: "Blasphemous as it may seem, the same logic that drives the Holy Communion in the Catholic Church drives consumer behavior in the market place. Through consuming American symbols, we become part of and empowered by the most powerful Archetype and Myth of all times: the American Dream."[61]

Marketing's adoption of storytelling therefore goes far beyond a mere shift in the way brands are promoted. Storytelling implies a "worldview" and projects it on to the whole of society. According to Stephen Denning, it is not just a marketing tool but a managerial "discipline."[62] Denning was one of the first to begin to experiment with storytelling techniques in the mid 1990s. For that is where it all began...

2   The Invention of Storytelling Management

On June 12, 2005, Steve Jobs, the legendary boss of Apple computers, addressed the students of Stanford University: "I am honored to be with you at your commencement from one of the finest universities in the world. I never graduated from college. Truth be told, this is the closest I've ever gotten to a college graduation. Today I want to tell you three stories from my life. That's it. No big deal. Just three stories."[1]

A Story For Our Times

The first story was the *Bildungsroman* of Apple's founder: the story of a poor kid who was left to his own devices and who, more or less by accident, enrolled in a typography course (it was thanks to this training that the Mac became the first personal computer to have a bitmap font). The second was a story of love and loss: the legend of how the first Macintosh was created in his parents' garage and then, over the next ten years, the success story of Apple and Jobs' meeting with his future wife, with whom he would start a family. But, no sooner had he won than he was the hero excluded from his own success. He had to leave the company he had founded. The third is a story of death and resurrection: Steve Jobs miraculously survived a diagnosis of pancreatic cancer. At the end of his story, the hero recovers his health and wins back the company he founded and which he will lead to new success.

Steve Jobs ended his short story with the advice he had read in a children's magazine as a boy: "Stay hungry, stay foolish." There was, of course, nothing spontaneous about this performance. When he told his stories, Apple's boss was conforming to the norms established by storytelling's intrusion into the spheres of management ten years earlier. That is a different story, and it is one worth telling.

It is a story for our times. It is an edifying story, with the stars of the new economy in the leading roles: Steve Jobs, Richard Branson, Bill Gates, and many others, directors of the World Bank, IBM, Xerox, and the gurus who preach "capitalism with soul."[2] It is a true story that tells us of "lean" multinationals that turned away from production to develop daring screenplays that made their shares soar on the Stock Exchanges, of international organizations on which the health of millions of people in Africa depends, and whose directors sometimes have difficulty communicating from one office to another. It is a story that tells of "battles with organizational monsters" in glass towers in New York, where hyper-motivated managers try to persuade their colleagues to accept "daring transformations" and to transform profoundly their perception of both themselves and their company. They are, explains French management consultant Dominique Christian, "stories of miraculous strategic virtuosity and heroic turnarounds … Stories of the heroes and heroines who make success possible."[3] They are stories that celebrate the "knowing firm" whose object is no longer just to produce commodities, but to share knowledge, to circulate information, and to manage emotions.

This is also the story of the invention of storytelling management. This new school of management emerged in the United States in the 1990s, and it recommends bringing storytellers and griots into companies. There are many new lessons to be learned: thinking, acting, networking, managing distance, forming nomadic teams, mastering the information overload, adapting to the speed of real-time business... There are innovations that lead to "e-transformations"[4] and stubborn prejudices that cost companies millions of dollars. PowerPoint presentations, checklists, and boring arguments have had their day. Make way for storytelling!

According to Steve Denning, a former World Bank director and now one of the new management's most active gurus, it is easy to explain the success of storytelling in the mid 1990s: "The origin of my interest in organizational storytelling was simple: nothing else worked."[5]

The Silence of the Start-Ups

What is the common factor linking the explosion that destroyed the Challenger space shuttle, the crisis at the *New York Times*, and the financial scandals at Enron, Tyco Electronics, WorldCom, and Health-South?

According to the Concours Group and Vitalsmarts, a group of consultants specializing in crisis management, these organizations, which experienced serious difficulties in 2003, were all part of the same "culture of silence." According to Vitalsmart's President Joseph Grenny, all these failures could have been avoided if these organizations had paid attention to one crucial attribute of their cultures: "the way in which they manage crucial conversations."[6]

Another study by the same group of consultants, published in February 2007 and entitled *Silence Falls*, hammers home the same point. Some 1,000 directors from 40 or so companies were surveyed, and the study looked at 2,200 industrial projects in sectors as diverse as the pharmaceutical industry, financial and banking services, government agencies, and consumer products. It reached the surprising conclusion that "organizational silence" is the cause of 80 percent of failed business programs and projects.[7]

"Is silence killing your company?" asked Harvard Professor of Leadership Leslie A. Perlow in March 2003, after spending some time immersed in the world of start-ups, the mutant companies that expanded so rapidly thanks to the Internet explosion.[8] It all began when Netscape was floated on the Stock Exchange in 1995 and lasted until the dotcoms collapsed from April 2000 onwards. Perlow spent nineteen months in a start-up founded by three students and studied it as though she was "an anthropologist studying a foreign culture." She was able to observe the company's life cycle, from its successful launch—after a few months, its value was estimated at $125 million—until its final bankruptcy. According to her, the reasons for the failure of so many start-ups were not purely financial or the result of the sudden bursting of a speculative bubble related to computer technology and telecommunications. The reasons also had to be sought in the silence of their directors, their inability to communicate with partners, in the things that were left unsaid and in unresolved conflicts: "Our research shows that silence is not only ubiquitous and expected in organizations but extremely costly to both the firm and the individual,"[9] and that its effects can range from simple misunderstandings to the bankruptcy of the organizations concerned.

In companies that made a cult of communications and whose essential task was to facilitate the exchange of information on the Internet, collaborators at all levels of the hierarchy proved to be incapable of communicating with one another, of dealing with disagreement, and of handling conflict. A worrying "silence" was undermining the dot-coms from within. It was the stock-market spiral that that swept them away, but there was also an internal spiral. Following the German sociologist Elisabeth Noelle-Neumann, Perlow described it as a "spiral of silence":

> Silence is associated with many virtues: modesty, respect for others, prudence, decorum. Thanks to deeply ingrained rules of etiquette, people silence themselves to avoid embarrassment, confrontation, and other perceived dangers. The social virtues of silence are reinforced by our survival instincts ... The need for quiet submission is exaggerated by today's difficult economy where millions of people have lost their jobs and many more worry that they might.[10]

Extending her study to other sectors, she concluded that silencing conflicts was a universal problem in companies, whatever their size or form, and that employees had great difficulty in identifying this dangerous syndrome before it had disastrous effects. "Our interviews with senior executives and employees ranging from small businesses to Fortune 500 corporations reveal that silence can exact a high psychological price on individuals, generating feelings of humiliation, pernicious anger, resentment, and the like, that, if unexpressed, contaminate every interaction, shut down curiosity and undermine productivity." Along the way, she found that everyone had a story to tell at every level of the organizations' hierarchies.

A History of Silence

Why is neo-management interested in what workers have to say? Could they have discovered that silence at work is a new source of waste, like slack periods, absenteeism, and sabotage? Do these worries concern all categories of wage-earners and all sectors of activity? The history of this odd couple—silence and work—needs to be written. The silence of the craftsman concentrating on his task is deliberate and sovereign. Silence can be enforced by the disciplines imposed by a foreman or by the noise of machinery. The silence of factories and workshops can block the expression of complaints and demands, and the transmission of skills. There is a link between fear and silence.

Bernard Girard, who has written a history of management theories, reminds us that, as early as the eighteenth century, Mandeville had noted that the silence of the British, as opposed to the noise made by the French, gave the British workforce a competitive advantage: "The silence that reigns in English factories and the way they do business, promptly and keeping their appointments, impresses all visitors."[11] The way the factories were organized was based on a military model. The military schools, which had been turned into industrial schools run by former officers, introduced military discipline into the world of production: their pupils wore uniforms, were recruited into battalions that drilled in the factory yard, were woken by the sound of drums and were forced to be silent in the workshops ... At the end of the century, we will see them again in Henri Fayol's projects.

On visiting an English factory in 1859, Louis Reybaud noted: "Two things strike one more than anything else: the small number of people employed and the silence that reigns."[12] Forty years earlier, Charles Dupin wrote: "When one enters these establishments, one is struck by the general order they exhibit. The workers are busily active, almost always in silence."[13] Without retracing the history of management here,[14] we will simply recall that silence at work became the rule when the factory emerged: many different labor forces were brought together in the same place and subjected to a very hierarchical discipline in which verbal exchanges inside the factory were strictly controlled.

The same interdiction applied to the women who worked in shops and offices. In 1898, one sales assistant told *La Fronde* newspaper:

This is our lot: we must accept wages that are not enough to live on, and keep silent; we have to stand, which becomes unbearable after a few hours, and keep silent. After an exhausting day, we must stay awake when and how our masters wish us to remain awake, and keep silent. We must put up with the improper remarks of passers-by, the crude suggestions of our bosses, and keep silent. When we are ill, we must put on a pleasant face and keep silent. We must keep silent, keep silent if we do not want to be dismissed.

Le Père Peinard, for its part, commented: "There poor women could not be more silent if you sewed their lips up."[15]

"In the cigarette factories of about 1870," writes Marie-Victoire Louis, women workers did not have the right to speak or smile. The same applied in the Galeries Lafayette in 1914, when they were also forbidden to address each other with the familiar *tu*. In the Parlerie in Périgueux in 1925, there was a complete ban on talking, and also on singing: "The women have to work all day long in an absolute silence that is broken only by the noise of the objects they need to perform their tasks."

In *Discipline and Punish*, Michel Foucault traces how the silence of workers spread from military schools to industrial schools, from barracks to workshops and factories, from armies to prisons. It spread throughout the disciplinary society like a lava flow. Foucault lists its instruments and techniques, but also its rites and codes: the internal regulations of workshops, barracks, and schools, which codified the right to speech, ritualized its written or oral forms, and authorized or banned its expression. This enforced silence is a basic element of the early management theories of Ford and Fayol. It spreads to the Fordist factory. In the twentieth century, the speech of workers, which was described as chatter or gossip, was seen as a distraction, a relaxation of discipline or even a form of passive "resistance": workers who talked were suspected of plotting stoppages and strikes. Work on the assembly line reduces the workplace to silence; the noise of the machines replaces the talk of the workers. In direct contrast, strikes and factory occupations were, throughout the twentieth century, identified with speech, and any return to work was seen as a return to compulsory silence.

From the Industrial Revolution onwards, silence was one of the arsenal of measures that gave managers control over their labor force. And the same silence still reigns in many places. In the outsourced workshops of Indonesia, China, and Brazil, as in the factories of the developed countries, on assembly lines and in sweatshops, workers' ability to speak is still subject to a discretionary power. And not only there: as we have seen, silence also reigns in start-ups and dotcoms, in the offices of insurance companies and in boards of directors, behind the screens of Silicon Valley's computer firms and in the glass towers of financial giants like Enron and WorldCom, where pension funds build up and evaporate.

"Don't Keep Quiet: Tell Stories"

But does this silence always have the same meaning? Of course not. Ever since the 1990s, management theorists have been forced to deal with the question of what they call "organizational silence" or "systematic silence." As Elizabeth Wolfe Morrison and Frances J. Milliken explain:

> We argue that there are powerful forces in many organizations that cause widespread withholding of information about potential problems or issues by employees. We refer to this collective-level phenomenon as "organizational silence." In our model we identify contextual variables that create conditions conducive to silence and explore the collective sense-making dynamic that can create the shared perception that speaking up is unwise. We also discuss some of the negative consequences of systemic silence, especially for organizations' ability to change and develop in the context of pluralism.[16]

When Enron collapsed in 2003, the world of management had to explain, to its great embarrassment, that one of the new economy's flagships was nothing more than a mirage or a financial fiction: this bankruptcy showed that silence could lead to phenomena of collective blindness. Within the space of a few months, millions of retired people lost everything they had. The company's directors were indicted for having lied to their employees and shareholders. According to Californian academic David Boje, "Enron made the narrative bluff that Washington politicians and Wall Street analysts would not be able to distinguish between fiction and reality."[17]

Hence, in contrast, the new virtues that are attributed to those who break the silence. In 2002, three women were named as *Time* magazine's "personalities of the year." Their exploits were described as "whistle-blowing." All three had chosen to break the law of silence that reigned in their organization. Cynthia Cooper, vice-president of WorldCom, had pointed out to her board of directors that the irregularities in its accounts amounted to $4 billion. Enron's vice-president Sherron Watkins had alerted her CEO Ken Lay shortly before the company went bankrupt. FBI agent Colleen Rowley had handed her superiors a file on Zachariah Moussaoui who, before 9/11, had denounced the inadequacies of the American secret services in an eleven-page report.[18]

Why are company employees being asked to break the silence, when they have been forced to remain silent for so long? How are they be convinced that what was once a proof of loyalty and discipline has now become an obstacle to change and innovation? Does this hold out the promise of a new social democracy? Whatever the reason, there has been a complete reversal: according to the neo-management gurus, employees should not be forced to keep silent. On the contrary, they should be encouraged to break the silence, to speak out, and to tell their stories. Whatever their age, competence, skills, and responsibilities, they all have "a story to tell." And the organization is interested in those stories.

Management theorists' change of attitude with respect to silence within organizations began in the 1980s. As early as 1984, James March and Gujme Sevon had recognized the merits of gossip. In a co-authored study of storytelling techniques in business, Nicole Giroux describes gossip as a form of narration that conveys information. According to this view, this elementary way of swapping stories "helps to maintain the system by communicating its rules and values and by disseminating the organization's traditions and history."[19] The educational virtues of story-telling have also been identified in a study of the "memorable messages" retained by newcomers to the company. As Nicole Giroux explains, the power of narration lies in its ability to capture "complex experiences" that combine the senses, reason, emotions, and the imagination into a dense résumé that can be reconstructed on the basis of any part of it.[20]

Between 1987 and 1990, the industrialist anthropologist Julian Orr carried out a series of studies of the workers responsible for repairing photocopiers at Xerox. Theirs was a small world of technical documentation, machines, and technicians who could mobilize phenomena and explain them in complex words, but there were also repairmen and maintenance staff, who did not have those skills. Orr demonstrated that swapping stories was central to the diagnostic process. In this world, the process of collective narration gradually led to a shared diagnosis of the situation.

When it comes to storytelling management, David Boje is, however, the precursor with his 1991 study of storytelling performance in an office-supply firm. The analysis of 12 hours of taped interviews allowed him to identify eleven scenarios. Boje found that the narrative activity of a group or organization does not take the form of structured narratives that are passed on by narrators to passive listeners. People tell their stories in fragments and are constantly interrupted by colleagues who add elements drawn from their own experience. The outcome is a collective form of narration. It is polyphonic but it is also discontinuous and made up of interwoven fragments, of histories that are talked about and swapped. They can sometimes be contradictory, but the company becomes a storytelling organization whose stories can be listened to, regulated, and, of course, controlled. Silent firms like Enron or WorldCom are contrasted with the symmetrical model of a firm that is talkative and voluble, and that tells stories.[21]

Management Theorists and the "Narrative Turn"

As Thierry Boudès, who teaches at the Ecole Supérieure de Commerce explains, "the 'narrative turn' of the 1990s came about because management researchers made the simple discovery that companies are microcosms in which lots of stories are produced and circulated."[22] The canteen, for example, is the classic site for this spontaneous production of narrative. But narration is also a central part of a company's activity, from reports on visits to clients to recruitment interviews (after all, a CV is simply a form of autobiographical story). "Storytelling management" is nothing more than attempt to control the way these stories evolve.

Rather than putting up with the flow of the stories that are anarchically produced within the company, storytelling management attempts to exploit and control it by introducing systematized forms of in-house communications and management based upon the telling of anecdotes. According to Boudès, "Storytelling is also a form of action. Narratives circulate within companies at least as easily as electrons, and they are a valuable way of transmitting experience. It is not by accident that we speak of 'success stories'. Swapping stories is one way of making a worldview intelligible and, therefore, sharing it. A story is not a servile photograph of an external reality; it helps to structure that reality."[23]

In the early 1990s, Steve Denning was tasked by the World Bank with improving the circulation and sharing of knowledge and information. The World Bank's missions are at once financial and advisory: it has to finance development projects, but it also has to circulate good ideas and transfer knowledge and experience. Several internal reports (1988, 1989, 1993, and 1995) had stressed the need to define a policy and procedures to control the management of information. They all came to the same conclusion: the information system no longer met the organization's needs. The information stored in its silos seemed inaccessible to most employees. Steve Denning sent out memo after memo and organized conference after conference, but they met with general indifference. He found that rational arguments no longer made any impact on its staff and that traditional communications methods — memos, conferences, Power-Point presentations, checklists, etc. — were ineffective, even though the volume and flow of information was constantly increasing and circulating faster than ever.

It was at this point that a colleague told him about a nurse in a small town 370 miles from the capital of Zambia who had been looking for information on how to treat malaria and found what she needed on the website of the Centers for Disease Control in Atlanta. The story revealed what now seems obvious: thanks to the Internet, knowledge and skills can be transmitted from an American laboratory to a nurse in a rural area on the other side of the world. But what worried Denning was that the World Bank, which had a mission to transfer knowledge, had played no role in this story. The story was simple, and easily told: it illustrated both the problem and the solution, and could very easily be transmitted to any organization.

Denning decided to include the "Zambian story" in his arsenal of arguments. To his great surprise, it spread throughout the whole organization. His Zambian story made it possible to change the image of the World Bank, which had often been criticized for its inefficiency. If the organization was capable of arranging knowledge transfers from rich countries to poor countries, its actions would no longer be seen as purely financial, and it would take on the features of the nurse who had to resolve a public health issue.

Steve Denning left the World Bank at the end of the 1990s. Convinced that he had found a communications method that could revolutionize companies, he became one of the storytelling management movement's most active "gurus." His Zambian story has become a classic in storytelling training sessions. He has told it thousands of times. Rejecting the over-rational traditional managerial approach, which he describes as "Napoleonic," he advocates a Tolstoyian approach, which is the only technique that can take account of the "richness and complexity of living" and of establishing "connections between things." He has published several books in which he refers to Roland Barthes' narratology, but he is also quite happy to make up animal fables like the story of "Squirrel Inc." Every year, the company loses 50 percent of its store of nuts because its leadership is not based upon storytelling.[24]

Telling Stories About Work

"I've always had a thing about campfires, never liked ghost stories, or singing *Blowing in the Wind*," Lucy Kellaway wrote in the eminently serious *Financial Times* on May 10, 2004; "But the juxtaposition of 'campfire' and 'corporate' is truly terrifying."[25] The *FT* writer's irony was directed at Evelyn Clark's book *Around the Corporate Campfire*.[26] Clark is a professional on the new "storytellers" circuit and recommends the use of storytelling in management. Her website, which boasts a logo showing a flute player charming a snake, tells visitors that "Evelyn Clark, the Corporate Storyteller" helps organizations to "develop red-hot and value-based stories that spread like wild fire and propel [managers] towards their vision."

Kellaway comments: "The thought that anyone who writes so badly could be let loose on a story is alarming, especially if the stories they are after are 'red-hot' and 'value-based'." Her article, entitled "Once Upon A Time, We Had Managers, Not Storytellers," is very much the exception within the extensive hagiographic literature on the use of storytelling in company management. A simple Internet search carried out in June 2007 gave some idea of the extent of the craze: Google found 20.2 million mentions of storytelling, and 719,000 of digital storytelling.

Storytelling management (STM) has in fact been a huge success; it has been adopted by major companies like Disney, McDonald's, Coca-Cola, Adobe, IBM, and Microsoft. It regularly makes the headlines of the *Harvard Business Review*, *The Economist* and the *Wall Street Journal*, and it has won over the managers of *Fortune*'s top 500 firms. There are bestsellers, articles, blogs, and websites devoted to it. Storytelling festivals began to be held all over the United States in the wake of the legendary National Storytelling Festival, first held in Jonesborough, Tennessee in 1972. Their audiences grow larger by the year and are very diverse, including laid-back hippies, yuppies, therapists, lawyers, video-game designers, and managers, all drawn to the powers ascribed to their likeable and bearded storytelling bards, who were once content to travel around like folk singers as they told the stories they had dashed off in a hurry.

Benedikt Benenati was one of the first to introduce storytelling management in France when he worked at Danone in 2003. As the weekly business magazine *Stratégies* reported in 2005: "A good story can be told in thirty seconds in the lift," Benedikt Benenati tells us. But first you have to loosen tongues. "It is not easy to overcome inhibitions in a very decentralized group that employs 80,000 people." In order to bring about this little revolution, he organizes "good ideas" fairs for managers, in which storytellers show what they have come up with. "For two hours, PowerPoint presentations are banned to encourage a return to simple, direct communications between people," he congratulates himself, before going on to talk about the video clips in which everyone tells the story of their ideas. Danone went one step further and published little collections of nice stories, complete with photos. We learn, for example, how Manuela Borella, the Spanish director of the Danao brand (a mixture of milk and fruit produced by a Danone subsidiary) increased her sales by 98 percent thanks to the advertising concept developed by her Saudi counterpart Omar Alsuleimani. The story of how a pair of twins were reconciled by Danone was another big hit in Spain. "These nice stories prove to everyone that swapping good ideas allows the group to make a good profit," comments Benenati in terms of approval.[27]

According to IBM France's head of internal communications Evelyne Gilbert, her company has developed the same interest in storytelling. In 2004, explains *Stratégies*:

> Four or five stories from salaried employees were posted on the Intra-net to mark the company's ninetieth birthday. "Everyone looked back at their life at IBM. A retired lady in Nantes even described how she had had to quickly hide strategic documents during the Second World War. An excellent way of immersing new recruits in the company's culture," boasted Evelyne Gilbert, who has a network of local corre-spondents whose job it is to bring her stories from the field. IBM's Intranet devotes two sections to storytelling. One talks about teams' fruitful experiments. The other traces the exemplary career of a company employee. The professional storyteller's key words are "per-sonalize" and "contextualize." IBM's managers have to tell stories to get their employees to accept the thousands of job losses in Europe recently announced by the company.[28]

This tacit knowledge circulates within the company in volatile forms: around the coffee machines and in the canteen, in corridors and stair-ways. The storytelling project boils down to a general story about life at work. The story becomes a management issue: coordination, interaction, sharing practices, getting ready for changes, sackings, innovations. Everyone is required to describe their experiences and to feed the story-machine that records, classifies, and formats their stories.

Chatter, stories, gossip, and rumors have acquired a new status. They are now seen as a vector for experiences and knowledge. A whole body of informal historical knowledge that has been shaped by experience can be crystallized, and so can the hitherto unrecognized forms of "tacit" knowledge without which the organization would be unable to function. The weekly *Jeune Afrique* gave an idyllic account of the process in 2006: "When applied in such different circumstances as handling major changes, mergers between companies, outsourcing and even sackings, storytelling allows ideas to evolve rapidly, mobilizes and motivates staff and does away with psychological blocks and tensions within a group."[29]

The *FT*'s Lucy Kellaway admits: "When I first came across the corporate storytelling craze about six or seven years ago, I thought it was a joke … I was quite wrong. Since then this craze has grown and grown. There turns out to be a huge industry of people with 'storyteller' or, worse, 'storyteller practitioner' written on their business cards, who make a living helping executives with their stories."[30]

The Magical Fables of Capitalism's Gurus

"Question: what do shamrocks, symphony orchestras, gazelles, federations, astronauts, atoms and molecules, schools of sharks, virtual networks, white-water rafting, jazz bands, diamonds and ant colonies have in common? Answer: Not much. But all of them have been invoked to describe the properties of a new organizational model that is replacing top-down bureaucratic machines."[31] The opening lines of Rosabeth Moss Kanter's 1997 bestseller are interesting on more than one count. These words from the former editor-in-chief of the *Harvard Business Review*, who is now a famous management guru, make it possible to date the emergence of a new form of management to the 1990s; the book locates the issues at the heart of the change experienced by the big companies that had to transform themselves as a result of the globalization of their markets. And it provides a good definition of the discursive style used by the management gurus.

Rosabeth Moss Kanter's list is indeed surprising. It is a totally chaotic muddle of species and activities, animals and associations, structures and networks, and turns its back on the rational order that had until then prevailed in the discourse of company directors. It is reminiscent of the Chinese encyclopedia cited by Jorge Luis Borges, in which it is written that "animals are divided into: (a) belonging to the Emperor, (b) embalmed, (c) tame, (d) sucking pigs, (e) sirens, (f) fabulous, (g) stray dogs, (h) included in the present classification, (i) frenzied, (j) innumerable, (k) drawn with a very fine camelhair brush, (l) *et cetera*, (m) having just broken the water pitcher, (n) that from a long way off look like flies."

Michel Foucault was very fond of this text, and cites it in the preface to his *The Order of Things*.[32] It both made him laugh and puzzled him. It made him laugh because it is quite impossible to understand this collection of unrelated things. And it puzzled him because its heteroclite vertigo defies reason and has a destructive effect on language itself, unlike utopias, which "although they have no real locality afford consolation [and] run with the very grain of language and are part of the fundamental dimension of the *fabula*."[33] What to say then of such a power to dissolve language when it attacks precisely that dimension of the *fabula*?

According to storytelling guru Steve Denning, the stories that are useful to business can be put into categories that are almost as absurd (though he does not share Borges' sense of humor): (a) stories to share knowledge, (b) stories that ignite action, (c) stories about what might happen in the future, (d) stories based on satire and taming the grapevine, (e) springboard stories, sparking the future through a story about the past, (f) stories that communicate who we are—people, (g) stories that communicate who we are—brands, (h) stories that transmit values, (i) stories that bridge the knowing–doing gap, (j) stories that embody tacit knowledge.

Dave Snowden, former director of IBM's Institute of Management and director of the Cyenfin Center for Organizational Complexity, has also attempted to identify the archetypes specific to company stories. Taking his inspiration from the Russian semiologist Vladimir Propp, who collected Russian folk tales in order to establish a set of structural functions specific to the folk tale,[34] he established a list of useful stories and effective fables. For anyone who has read Propp, the results are hair-raising. His list includes "the story of a market where everything is on sale, except honor," "the fable of the sweet little bear cubs who were transformed into battle-hardened warriors because of the dirty tricks played on them by their competitors," and the parable of "the jazz band in which everything always had to be reinvented." Then there is the metaphor of "the paths that were not chosen —what would have happened if you hadn't made this choice as opposed to another," and the story showing how "successes can be turned into failures, and failures into successes that no one recognizes," and the one that describes how "things happened differently by telling one person's story as though it was something that happened to someone else." There is the plot that "transforms competitors into friends, friends into competitors, heroes into bastards and bastards into heroes." There is also the legend of the company that succeeded, "despite the organized chaos," and of "the tension between the slave-drivers and the charismatic managers," and of "the squabbles between the teams that were like hostile tribes, each believing itself to be more important than the rest"; and not forgetting the "Marseillaise joke: everyone has to tell a story even more outrageous than that told by the last person."[35]

The irruption of storytelling gurus into a business world famed for its cult of efficiency and pragmatism—that justifies its actions by appealing to supposedly natural laws (the market, profit), that is characterized by its aggressive tautologies ("business is business"), and that respects only the law of economic performance—is symptomatic of an underlying phenomenon, which might be described as the business world's regression into the world of fables and fictions. The rise of storytelling in business is in any case inseparable from the "management guru" phenomenon. The term is recent and, according to David Greatbatch and Timothy Clark's book on how the gurus perform,[36] was first used to describe management consultants in an article in the *Sunday Times* in 1983; it coincides with the emergence of the phenomenon in the United States.

The term has become commonplace in the West, and its Indian origins—the Sanskrit word *guru*, which English has borrowed from Punjabi and Hindi, means "spiritual master"—have taken on a magical dimension that refers, more or less consciously, to Africa's griots. In Africa, the term "griot" refers not to a job or even a vocation, but to a social function. It is traditionally reserved for activities that develop on the fringes of accepted beliefs and knowledge, or in the field left vacant by medical or religious orders. Its efficacy—real or otherwise—has to do with the charisma of someone who is described as a griot, his gifts and prowess being manifested in a sort of self-revelation that is passed on by rumors or legends: unexplained cures, reconciliations between clans, and mediations between parties in conflict. In Mali, griots are described as *djéli*, which is Bambara for "blood of society." The *djéli* is a "bond doctor": his task is to reconcile, to sew up wounds by telling stories, which may be either true or fictional. Some griots are also journalists or mediators in strikes.

"We cannot consider the *djéli* outside our cultural context," explains Bakary Soumano, the *djéli* chief in the Bamako region of Mali. "We live in a hierarchical society that is divided into clans, but are descended from a common ancestor." The clans must sustain relations of solidarity, and the *djéli*'s role is to promote that solidarity. In order to do so, he begins by evoking the genealogy of the individuals in dispute and by reminding them of what united their clans in the past.[37]

The misunderstanding implicit in the appearance of the concept of "management gurus" in the America of the 1980s is therefore a good illustration of the slippage from a set of management tools and techniques that were to a greater or lesser extent inspired by the human sciences (social psychology, rhetoric, and linguistics), to practices that are legitimized by magical thought, and then storytelling. Denning writes: "When I saw how easily round-edged stories could slide into our minds, I found myself wondering whether our brains might not be hardwired to absorb stories."[38]

Gurus, Purveyors of Managerial Fashion

According to the British researchers Greatbatch and Clark:

Most of the leading management gurus are American. Given this situation it is possible that certain features of American society support the development of management gurus and guru theory. These could include the focus of a dream, an idealized sense of possibility, the assumption that individuals are adaptable to a dynamic and changing future, and the relatively poor performance of American organizations in the face of (mainly) Japanese and south-east Asian competition, especially in the 1980s.[39]

The main reason for the craze lies in the crisis that hit American companies at the end of the 1980s, when they were faced with competition from Japan and the Asian "dragons," and had to rethink the management techniques bound up with the old Fordist model.

Andrej Huczynski, a management specialist at the University of Glasgow, identifies three types of gurus: "academics," "consultants," and "manager heroes."[40] Academic gurus like Charles Handy, Gary Hamel, Rosabeth Moss Kanter, Michael Porter, and Peter Senge are products of a few famous business schools (London, Harvard, Sloan, Stanford, etc.). The "consultants" group is made up of independent advisers, writers, and commentators such as Peter Drucker, Michael Hammer, and Tom Peters. As for manager heroes like Bill Gates and Steve Jobs, their guru status has to do with their brilliant success in business. According to Huczynski, those management consultants who are regarded as gurus and who are famous for their performance and successful interventions represent only a tiny minority within their profession. They are included in lists established on the basis of different criteria (sales of bestsellers, the size of the companies they advise, the cost and number of their interventions).

The sales of the books they have published since the 1980s are indeed an astonishing publishing phenomenon. *In Search of Excellence* (Peters and Waterman, 1982), *The Seven Habits of Highly Effective People* (Covez, 1989), *When Giants Learn to Dance* (Kanter, 1989), *The Fifth Discipline* (Senge, 1990), and *Re-Engineering the Corporation* (Hammer and Champy, 1993), have sold several hundred thousand, if not millions, of copies. Such success is such an integral part of the gurus' strategy of conquest and self-legitimation that some authors (like Michael Hammer and James Champy[41]) have gone so far as to manipulate the *New York Times'* bestseller lists by getting people to buy multiple copies of their books from the stores that are used to establish the rankings.

The gurus' tours of the international lecture circuit are also an element in the reputation they enjoy in the eyes of their audience of managers. A good guru can earn several million dollars a year. In the 1980s, Tom Peters took part in 150 seminars a year and charged $60,000 for each appearance; during the first decade of the new century, he has restricted his appearance to 50 seminars a year and charges $70,000 to $90,000 for a half-day seminar. Gary Hamel, Rosabeth Moss Kanter, Michael Hammer, and Peter Senge charge the same. Tom Peters is rumored to earn $6 million a year for his appearances. It has been estimated that there are fifty or so global superstars for a worldwide market of just under $1 billion a year.[42]

The gurus are purveyors of managerial fashion. The popularity of their ideas comes and goes and has a life cycle of "invention" (when the idea is created), "dissemination" (when the idea is brought to the notice of a target audience), "support" (when the idea is accepted), and "disenchantment" (when negative evaluations and frustrations begin to emerge), at which point the idea either fades or is abandoned. According to Greatbatch and Clark, "a plethora of empirical studies have examined the diffusion patterns of fashionable guru-led discourses within the print media. Using citation analysis the number of references to a particular idea in a sequence of years are counted and plotted in order to identify the life-cycle of a fashionable management idea."[43]

These studies demonstrate that the time-gap between the appearance of a new managerial schema and its peak of popularity decreased considerably from 14.8 years in the period 1950–70 to 7.5 years in the 1980s, and 2.6 years in the 1990s. These ideas are created and spread by a network of consultant companies, business schools, and publishers, who are themselves in competition with one another. Their success with their managerial audience depends upon "the dissemination of ideas and techniques to the managerial audience."[44]

Many authors describe management gurus as expert persuaders who try to format their audience by means of effective speeches, and some even compare their oratorical powers to those of evangelical preachers.[45] But it took the work of Greatbatch and Clark (2005) to give us an accurate idea of how the storytelling gurus perform. Their study, which is based on tape and video recordings, reveals the purely rhetorical nature of the gurus' interventions (hence the book's subtitle "Why We Believe What Management Gurus Tell Us"):

> Tom Peters perhaps comes closest to the evangelical style ... Peters often adopts an aggressive and hectoring tone. He peppers his lectures with colloquialisms, profanities and hyperbole, uses exaggerated facial expressions and gestures, volume and pitch as he regales his audiences... He keeps audience members under constant surveillance, and is fond of gazing at individual audience members for prolonged periods of time, especially as he delivers key messages. Indeed, he is

known to prefer what is termed the "cocktail" arrangement (round tables with 10–15 people seated on each) for the auditoria in which he speaks. In this arrangement there is no stage and so he is free to roam the room and maintain direct contact with individual members of the audience. It is perhaps therefore not surprising that members of his audiences often look decidedly uncomfortable as Peters adopts a hectoring/aggressive style and looks directly at them, searching out the gaze of individual audience members.[46]

Peter Senge also interacts with his audience, but rarely gazes at individual audience members for prolonged periods of time; he "uses a more elevated, academic style of speaking, and frequently quotes other academics and philosophers, such as Kant and Searle."[47]

The gurus' stories last from twenty seconds to four minutes. The vast majority (87 percent) of their themes relate to daily life and to everyday activities that are, *a priori*, unlikely to fire their listeners' enthusiasm: eating in a restaurant, booking a hotel room, traveling, filling up the car with gas, driving, going to a management conference, and so on.[48]

As early as 1998, Clark and Salaman identified the three factors that determine the success of the gurus' performance.[49] They apparently have the effect of reducing psychological tension in managers who are confronted with a world that seems unstable, chaotic, and increasingly uncertain. They capture the spirit of the times and resonate with their audience's vague expectations. But the main reason for the gurus' success with managers has to do with the narrative form of their performances and their use of stories that inevitably celebrate management's merits and heroism. A guru does not have to convince his audience or offer any proof. His only authority comes from a set of practices that supposedly has beneficial results because he possesses some mysterious knowledge, a wisdom that cannot be communicated, or simply because his words put his audience under a spell. It derives, in other words, from his ability to conjure up at any given moment the desired emotions or opinions by using determinate narrative sequences.

"People don't want more information," writes Annette Simmons, who wrote one of the bestselling books on storytelling. "They are up to their eyeballs in information. They want *faith*—faith in you, in your goals, your success, in the story you tell. It is faith that moves mountains, not facts. Facts do not give birth to faith. Faith needs a story to sustain it—a *meaningful* story that inspires belief in you and renews hope that your ideas indeed offer what you promise."[50]

Hence the importance of practices of self-legitimation and self-validation: the guru *is* his performance. He is the source of his useful stories and their mysterious effects; he is a concentrate of his narrative competence. He is both the agent and the mediator, the transmitter and the message. He must convince you that all is in order, and in keeping with common sense and the laws of nature. He is not teaching you a technique, but transmitting a proverbial wisdom that cultivates popular common sense, appeals to the laws of nature, and evokes a mythical order.

Shakespeare on Management

The function of the fables and their morals, of the useful stories and efficacious fictions, is to supply legitimacy. Governments have always been able to exploit *belles lettres*, and literature rarely escapes the function of legitimizing power, be it political, military, or even judicial. In his analysis of the Dominici murder case, which attracted huge publicity in France in the 1950s, Roland Barthes detects a disturbing and corrupting alliance between the legal system and literature; he condemns this alliance because it confuses genres by putting the story of an event on the same level as an accusation brought against a human being: "Justice and literature have made an alliance. They have exchanged their old techniques, thus revealing their basic identity and compromising each other barefacedly."[51]

Storytelling management forges a similar alliance between literature and management. The good company manager owes it to himself to be an "extraordinary storyteller" with a dazzling talent. Rather than producing a balance sheet, performance indicators, or figures for operating profits or losses, he should tell his colleagues and employees stories. According to Robert McKee, a famous Hollywood screenwriter who, within the space of ten years, became a storytelling management guru, "Motivating people to reach the organization's stated goals is a big part of a CEO's job … To do that, he or she must engage their emotions, and the key to their hearts is a story."[52]

Management therefore often puts on the mask of fiction and tells philosophical tales, fables about animals, or children's stories. A rash of essays sing the praises of the new alliance between business and litera-ture. Real literature, fictional company. The great novels of the past are read in an attempt to resolve in-house communications problems or to shed light on the staff's "irrational" reactions. Paul Corrigan's bestselling *Shakespeare on Management*, for example, suggests that we should reread Shakespeare's tragedies to find leadership models and practical lessons in human resources management.[53]

Similarly, Robert A. Brawer goes back to the classics of American and English literature.[54] The famous reply of Herman Melville's Bartleby — "I would prefer not to" — is apparently an expression of resistance to routine and the established conventions of the workplace. David Lodge's *Nice Work* (1988) demonstrates the absurdity of divorcing the human sciences from business. Dos Passos' *The Big Money* (1936) looks at how the American dream is embodied in different individuals' stories, from Henry Ford's to that of an anonymous tramp, from an idealist's to that of an opportunist. The novel apparently illustrates the conflict between personal values and the organizations' materialist culture. Joseph Conrad's *Typhoon* (1903) shows that a real leader must have the virtue of moral integrity, while *The Canterbury Tales* are a brilliant illus-tration of fourteenth-century mercantilism (being a merchant's son, Chaucer was well aware that the law of the market rules the world). William Gaddis' *J.R.* (1975) foresees the irruption of company advertis-ing into public schools, while David Mamet's *Glengarry Glen Ross* (1985) demonstrates that a talented salesman can persuade us to buy things we neither need nor want in a perfect illustration of the new marketing, which regards selling as a theatrical performance and consumption as an exchange of experiences.

In similar vein, the volume *Myths, Stories, and Organizations* — edited by Gabriel Yiannis, one of organizational storytelling's master thinkers — reveals the renewed interest in the narrative approach to organizations: "Organizations are now regarded as possessing certain folkloristic and even mythological qualities such as proverbs, recipes, rituals, ceremo-nies, style, and legends ... Undoubtedly, they possess certain characters, such as heroes, fools, tricksters, and so forth, as well as plot elements such as accidents, deceptions, mistakes, punishments, coincidences, and conflicts, which can also be found in ancient myths."[55] Each chapter in the book takes as its starting point a legend, story, or fable and explores its contemporary significance in a world of globalization and hyperconsumption. *The Odyssey* is reread and revised for organizational purposes, and becomes a world of heroes and heroines, gods and goddesses, ghosts and monsters. Some chapters deal with the question of leadership in the face of terrorism, the position of women within the organization, the construction of identity, and the management of emotions. All these stories tell how the heroes of our times are building a new world.

As we shall see, this is a new world in which fiction penetrates business to such an extent that it gradually shapes a "new economy" with some very strange rules.

3   The New "Fiction Economy"

"It can be difficult to have your body in India but your mind in America at the same time." Ashim Ahluwalia's astonishing documentary *John & Jane* looks at Bombay's call centers. Whereas exile means that your mind is in your country of origin while your body is in the host country, outsourcing has created a new category of emigrants whose bodies are in India while their minds are in America. Ahluwalia explains: "I first heard about call centers in 2001. There had already been some TV documentaries and news reports on the subject, but most of these were occupied with business advantages and technological growth. Nobody seems to be curious about the kind of people who worked there."[1]

India's Call Centers and the Globalization of Minds

At night, Namrata, Vandana, and Oaref become Naomi, Osmond, and Nikki. They work in a call center and spend their nights — they work at night because of the time-difference — answering American consumers' calls to 1-800 numbers. Just like immigrants landing at Ellis Island, they have to change their names. And yet they have not left their own country or crossed any frontier. The frontier crosses them. Every night, they sit down in front of their screens and become American. "For me, the idea of virtual 'call agents' with fake identities seemed like science fiction. Who were these Indians who became 'Americans' at night?" asks Ahluwalia.[2]

This metamorphosis is not immediate. Adopting an American forename is not enough to make anyone an American. The candidates have to undergo several transformations, starting with the accent neutralization classes that take away their Indian accents. The number of such training courses on offer in India has exploded as the number of call centers increases and as European and American companies outsource their back office structures. As IDG News Service's Bangalore correspondent John Ribeiro explains:

> The new business in training staff in Western communications skills and etiquette has attracted a number of entrepreneurs, many of them former employees in the hospitality industry ... "The art is to ensure that the customer [in the UK] does not distinguish between a call that was taken in the UK and one that was taken in India," said Sudheesh Venkatesh, head of human resources at the IT and business support services subsidiary in Bangalore of Tesco PLC, a UK-based retailer.[3]

The courses on offer are designed to initiate individuals into the Western lifestyle and culture. They are courses in what the professional jargon terms "cross-cultural sensitivity," which in most cases means the phenomenon of acculturation. "For example, employees at Tesco are advised to be current on political developments and favourite UK sports, so that they can talk about these topics with customers."[4] Samit Mallal, who co-wrote the documentary *Bombay Calling* with Ben Addelman, confirms that "some employees memorize the baseball scores so as to be able to joke with their American clients."[5] But the best tools for globalizing minds are the American TV series in which the call center workers are steeped.

Globalization has increased the need for cross-cultural sensitivity courses designed for, amongst others, executives from multinational companies who require an introduction to the cultures, and lifestyles of the countries they visit. And yet, "Training non-Indians on Indian culture, value and manners is not big business," explains the director of a training firm in Bangalore: "The culture industry in Bangalore is mainly a one-way street, as most multinationals and outsourcing companies concentrate only on training Indian staff to operate in westernized culture."[6]

The Souls of the Outsourced

In 2006, some 350,000 Indian workers swapped their identities every night in return for much more than the average wage.[7] This is what has been called "the new Indian dream," and it has replaced the old dream of emigration. Joseph Confavreux produced the remarkable documentary series broadcast *High-Speed India [L'Inde à grande vitesse]* for the French radio station France-Culture in March 2007. He explains: "They do not necessarily dream of emigrating, as they did twenty years ago, but some become emigrants at home. During the working day, they live at a European rhythm (language, life style, but also the weather forecast in order to satisfy customers on the other side of the world) before suddenly reverting to an Indian rhythm."[8] These young people "are subsumed into the pseudo-American lifestyle they are forced to adopt — to the point that they undergo a fundamental transformation: they become the job," comments Indian strategy consultant Radjika Chadha.[9] "Bridging continents by telephone, they pitch products and soothe frayed consumer nerves. As they troubleshoot, they dream of America. What is it like to transport yourself to a remote land you've never even seen? How does it feel to live so far outside your own body?"[10]

Discussing Ahluwalia's *John & Jane*, the *Observer*'s Amelia Gentleman notes that: "From soap opera to Bollywood musical, from arthouse documentary to best-selling novel, the call center has ... been immortalized as a symbol of contemporary India."[11]

According to Chetan Bhagat, whose novel *One Night@The Call Center* spent six months on the bestseller lists, the call centers encapsulate "the tensions of a nation caught between two eras." The business is "the interface between the Indian influences of older generations and the western influence that younger Indians are exposed to. It is the melting pot where all cultural influences meet." As Makarand Paranjape, an English professor at Delhi's Jawaharlal Nehru University, explains, Bhagat's novel is "an attempt to eroticise the industry, an attempt to make it a culturally exciting place, hip and cool. Of course it's a bit of a fantasy: there is nothing glamorous about call centers; they are dehumanising, decultured places." Here, thousands of young male and female college graduates spent the night confined in close proximity (breaking down the traditional distance between the sexes), in US-time, in smart, modern offices, adopting alien American identities, performing mindless tasks but earning salaries larger than anything their parents could aspire to.[12]

The six workers described in Ahluwalia's documentary all present symptoms of personality distortion to some degree. After 14 hours of work, we see them abandoning their American identities in the early morning and, like Indian Cinderellas, reverting to what they are — Namrata, Vandana, and Oaref — and going home to sleep. What do they dream of during the day? Of *Desperate Housewives*, *Prison Break*, or Jack Bauer, the agent in *24 Hours*? The most impressive metamorphosis is that undergone by Naomi, a young Indian woman who bleaches her skin and dyes her hair to look like Marilyn Monroe. She speaks with an American accent, even outside working hours. "Blonde to her eyelashes, she speaks with a kind of cyborg Midwest accent: 'I'm totally very Americanized.'"[13]

Living by night under house arrest in great call centers filled with the hubbub of phone conversations, these new migrants travel through time, not space. They "teletravel" the continents. They emigrate into the virtual time of telephone networks. Trapped in a virtual world they know only from advertising brochures and TV series, these workers see their identities gradually merging into a fantasy America. "*John & Jane* is a film about the need for everyone to become a hybrid American. It's like that in India and I think the whole world is becoming like that. The film is about what it means to be Indian in the twenty-first century. They shape our taste and our aesthetics and in some way, without meaning to, they end up shaping our identities," says the film's director.

Certain writers from postcolonial countries unreservedly celebrate multiculturalism, the confusion surrounding identity and the emergence of a global ego that is the product of a montage or collage of heteroclite cultural elements, but they often overlook the effects of the cultural domination and symbolic violence that are at work in the formatting of identities and the neutralization of singularities. Ahluwalia's film describes the other side of this economic and financial outsourcing: the temporal and cultural migration of what he calls the "souls of the outsourced." The director shot his film in 35 mm, which is the format used for full-length fictional films, and some scenes appear to have been scripted. Some viewers actually think that it is not a documentary but a work of fiction. According to the director, this ambiguity is deliberate: "It is a documentary because everything is real, but I like that you have to question whether it's reality or fiction."

The "Fictionalization" of Workplace Relations

The new management techniques, write Luc Boltanski and Eve Chiapello in *The New Spirit of Capitalism*, "are dependent less on procedures or mechanisms involving objects (as with the assembly line) than on people, and *the use of resources they make requiring their physical presence, their emotions, their gesticulations, their voice, and so on*."[14] It would be hard to put it better. "Adaptability," they go on, " —that is, the ability to treat one's own person *in the manner of a text that can be translated into different languages* —is in fact a basic requirement for circulating in networks, guaranteeing the transit through heterogeneity of a being minimally defined by a body and the proper noun attached to it."[15]

Curiously enough, the authors never refer to call centers, but when they attempt to identify the ideal-types of the new management that emerged in the 1990s, they do use words that describe very accurately the concrete experience of those who work in them. The globalization of markets and outsourcing do make individuals experience an unbearable tension between the need to adapt to a changing environment and the need to assert their identity, between flexibility and individualism. This neo-management therefore has to meet their contradictory demands for autonomy and interdependence. This presupposes less hierarchy and more control. It presupposes forms of behavior that allow its agent enough autonomy to adapt to complex and unpredictable situations within the framework of a scenario that constrains them.

This is a *mimetic* or fictional economy, as opposed to the libidinal economy described by Jean-François Lyotard. Its goal is to manipulate drives and emotions in order to produce and circulate behavioral models and imitative tendencies. "We call *the ideology that justifies engagement in capitalism* 'spirit of capitalism' … with the proviso that the ideology of capitalism is not reduced to meaning 'a moralizing discourse, intended to conceal material interests, which is constantly contradicted by practice', but in the sense that the work of Louis Dumont defines it as 'a set of shared beliefs, inscribed in institutions, bound up with actions, and hence anchored in the real.' "[16]

The authors do not evoke the role storytelling plays in the theories and techniques of this neo-management (partly because their research stops in the 1990s, but also because of their choice of a corpus of texts in French; it is only recently that French writers have noticed the existence of storytelling). Their analyses do, on the other hand, help to explain its rise. In the early 1980s, the figure of the junior executive gave way to that of the manager, then that of the leader or "coach," and finally that of the storyteller whose stories speaks to our hearts and not just our reason by supplying visions of the company and the fictions that allow it to *function*. "Neo-management literature must therefore demonstrate how the prescribed way of making profit might be desirable, interesting, exciting, innovatory or commendable."[17]

In the course of his investigations into the sectors of high technology, high finance, and urban services, the American sociologist Richard Sennett also observed the growing "fictionalization" of relations in the workplace. Neo-management's response to increasingly fierce competition is the fiction that "employees aren't really competing against each other. And even more important, the fiction arises that workers and bosses aren't antagonists; the boss instead manages group process. He or she is a 'leader,' the most cunning word in the modern management lexicon."[18]

The American anthropologist Charles Darrah's work on "human skills" training in high-tech manufacturing companies confirms the fiction of teamwork. "For instance, Vietnamese workers who composed about 40 percent of the workforce in one company were 'especially fearful of the team concept, which they likened to Communist work teams' … Employees learned the portable skills of teamwork through coaching in how to act various company roles, so that every worker would know how to behave in the varied windows of work."[19]

When she worked on the assembly line at a Subaru-Isuzu plant, the sociologist Laurie Graham "found the 'team metaphor was used at all levels of the company' … She found that people were oppressed in a particular way by the very superficiality of the fictions of teamwork … the fiction of cooperating employees served the company's drive for ever greater productivity … Subaru-Isuzu uses this fiction of community at work to help justify its fierce resistance to labor unions; moreover the fiction of community helps justify the existence of a Japanese company extracting profits in America to be sent home."[20] As Sennett comments, "To put this more formally, power is present in the superficial scenes of teamwork, but authority is absent."[21]

Emotional Capitalism's New Authority Model

The authority of a story—the story of "change"—has taken the place of power. This is a story written by the market, which uses as many pseudonyms as Pessoa uses heteronyms: internationalization, globalization, technical advances, competition... Power is absent, as in Lars von Trier's film *Le Direktor*, in which the boss of a computer company who is unwilling to let his employees see him taking any responsibility hires an actor to play his role. " 'People need to recognize we are all contingent workers in one form or another,' says the manager at ATT during a recent spate of downsizing; 'We are all victims of time and place.' "[22]

As we can see, one authority model is being replaced by another. The authority of the director has to give way to that of a story, and the company is nothing more than the way it is told, or a score that is conducted by management. Management techniques are beginning to look more and more like those of a theatrical director; partners have to adapt as best they can to their roles in order to make the story look credible to an audience of consumers and investors. The technical synchronization of flows of raw materials and labor power inside the company is giving way to a synchronization based on a story about everyone's roles and attributes, about their abilities and their useful emotions. In this context, narrative techniques that can keep a reader in suspense can do more than the old repertoires of taboos and constraints to involve the company's partners and get them to accept the story of a "change" they desire. "Many of those working in the new economy wanted to believe in more than business. For them, the new economy isn't primarily a financial institution. It's a creative institution. Like painting and sculpting, business can be a venue for personal expression and artistry,"[23] writes the British geographer Nigel Thrift. And as Boltanski and Chiapello note, neo-management has developed "mechanisms ... based upon consent and agreement [that] can achieve their objective only by merging with forms that possess the typical features of a grammar of authenticity: spontaneous, friendly relations; trust; requests for help or advice; attentiveness to sickness or suffering; friendship, even love."[24]

How can anyone turn down an invitation to be *authentic*? But how can we fail to notice that the only point of being authentic is to promote the best interests of the company?

Those who are caught up in the mechanisms cannot categorically refuse to participate in these exchanges ... But nor ... can they be unaware that these more "authentic" relations are reliant on techniques of mobilization ... Their emotions ... end up interfering with the strategic use they make of themselves and always risk exceeding it, almost without them being aware of it, as when people pass from an emotion that was initially obligatory, and which they thought affected, to a genuine emotion that grips and overwhelms them quite unexpectedly.[25]

"Capitalism has, they say, a cold face," writes Eva Illouz in *Cold Intimacies*, which reprints the "Adorno Lectures" she gave in Frankfurt in 2006. According to Illouz, who teaches sociology at the Hebrew University of Jerusalem, industrial capitalism is being transformed into an "emotional capitalism" that appropriates affects to such a degree that emotions are turned into commodities. "In the culture of emotional capitalism, emotions have become entities to be evaluated, bargained, inspected, quantified and commodified ... They have also contributed to creating a suffering self, that is, an identity organized and defined by its psychic lacks and deficiencies, which is incorporated back into the market by incessant injunctions to self-change and self-realization."[26]

That is why neo-management's prescriptions often adopt, as Boltanski and Chiapello remark, "a lyrical, even heroic style ... numerous references to noble and ancient sources such as Buddhism, the Bible and Plato, or to contemporary moral philosophy (Habermas in particular)."[27] As we saw in the last chapter, Homer, Shakespeare, Herman Melville, and Joseph Conrad can now be added to the list.

Fictions About Companies or Fictional Companies?

Don DeLillo's 1977 novel *Players* is about a company called the Grief Management Council: "Grief was not the founder's name; it referred to intense mental suffering, deep remorse, extreme anguish, acute sorrow and the like."[28] Grief Management caters for new needs and is interested in territories previously overlooked by the market: the deserts of pain and torment, the scorched earth of despair and mourning. This fictional company anticipates in astonishing fashion the personal services companies that mushroomed in the 1990s: its "clinics, printed material and trained counsellors served the community in its efforts to understand and assimilate grief."[29] Grief Management was as much concerned with physical suffering as moral suffering and published all sorts of educational brochures, offering courses for social or professional groups, and seminars for unhappy couples.

"He'd be so funny when he talked about his job and those people in the field. The stories. Do you believe? Per diem rates for terminal-illness counseling? So if it drags on, forget it, we got you by the balls? And the woman in Syracuse? With the grief-stricken pet, what was it, canary, in Syracuse, that the other one died ..."[30] DeLillo's irony is directed against capitalist societies' tendency to transform all emotions, including the most intimate feelings, such as mourning, remorse, or depression, into commodities. It may have looked overstated in 1977, but "Somebody anticipated that people would one day crave the means to codify their emotions."[31]

Five years later, in 1982, the management gurus Peters and Waterman wrote in their bestselling *In Search of Excellence*: "All that stuff you have been dismissing for so long as the intractable, irrational, informal organization can be managed ... what our framework has done is to remind the world of professional managers that soft is hard."[32]

At Grief Management, flexibility is the rule:

> The number of employees varied, sometimes radically, from month to month ... Making things seem even more fleeting was the fact that office space at Grief Management was constantly being reapportioned. Workmen sealed off some areas with partitions, opened up others, moved out file cabinets, wheeled in chairs and desks. It was as though they'd been directed to adjust the amount of furniture to levels of national grief.[33]

Its head office is in the World Trade Center. "Where else could you stack all this grief?" asks Pammy, who writes brochures for the company. "To Pammy, the towers didn't seem permanent. They remained concepts, no less transient for all their bulk than some routine distortion of light."[34]

These lines were written twenty-five years before the Twin Towers collapsed, and before architects proposed replacing them with purely visual phenomena and luminous fictions traced by laser beams. The visionary power of the novel is not, however, restricted to this prophetic remark. Grief Management prefigures the new company that would, in the 1990s, replace the old Fordist model, with its division of labor, its assembly lines, its hierarchical organization, its paternalist management, and its mountains of commodities, whose "immense accumulation" was, for Marx, one of the distinguishing features of the capitalist mode of production.

The fall of the Berlin Wall, the rise of finance capitalism facilitated by the conservative revolutions of Ronald Reagan and Margaret Thatcher, the globalization of markets, the emergence of new producers in Japan and South-East Asia, and the explosion of the Internet and new information technologies, have completely changed the conditions in which companies produce and optimize their profits. After a cycle of rapid growth (*les trente glorieuses*, or "the Golden Age of the Long Boom") based upon a relatively stable form of organization (the Fordist company), capitalism entered a zone of turbulence at the beginning of the 1980s. Management then began to look for a new paradigm that could give leaders a sense of where they were going in a period of profound readjustments that affected management and administration techniques, productive practices, the perimeter of companies, as well as the symbolic discourses and constructions they inspired.

As it made the transitions from the old craft-based factories to the giant bureaucracies of the Fordist era, and from nimble, decentralized Japanese firms to the logo companies of the "new economy," management experienced the revolutions embodied in the names Fayol, Taylor, Ford, Ohno, and many others. But the last revolution to date—whose emblematic authors include Bill Gates, Phil Knight, and Richard Branson—invokes surprising inventors who are neither engineers nor financiers but novelists. As we saw in the last chapter, the managerial revolution celebrated by the storytelling gurus refers not to Toyota, but to Tolstoy. Its ideal-type is no longer the industrial or commercial company, or even the financial firm, and nor is it the dematerialized logo company of the 1980s. It is a company that produces useful fictions, and can therefore be described as a *fiction company*.

Don DeLillo's novel identified with remarkable lucidity the ideal of a postindustrial company that was flexible, nimble, organized into networks, and designed to satisfy immaterial needs, be they cultural or human. Grief Management allows us to identify the three elements that would structure the new capitalism's rhetoric from the 1990s onwards:

- the first of these elements (its ethos, if you like) takes the form of a constant injunction to change;
- the second (its pathos) concerns the management of emotions and is part of the general process of manipulation and commodification that accompanies the construction of capitalism's new "subject" (consumer, wage-earner, or manager) as an emotional ego;
- the third (its logos) emphasizes the role of language, especially the use of stories, to manage that emotional ego.

It is thus a work of fiction that diagnosed the organizational crisis and the principles behind company reconstruction, long before the sociologists of labor and the management theorists did so. This reflects not only the genius of the novelist in question, but also the nature of the transformations that are taking place and the growing importance of the narrative function and fiction as agents of change within companies. Confronted with what has become an uncertain environment, the new company that emerged in the 1990s must be prepared to accept change and must be willing to exploit all possibilities. The prevailing state of mind might be described as novelistic because it presupposes an attitude that is characteristic of fictional worlds. The new economy's ideal-type is the suspension of disbelief that DeLillo captures so well in the phrase: the "need to feel you're on the verge of a wonderful change":

> "I am on the verge of a wonderful change. I am about to do something electrifying. The very fibers of your being will be electrified, sir, when I tell you what it is I propose to do." To speak it in words is to see the possibility emerge. Doesn't matter what. Don't bother your head over that. For the purposes of this discussion it could be mountain-climbing we're talking about or this friend of Jack, the oft-mentioned scaly chap who plans to swim the North Sea left-handed. Our lives are enriched by these little blurbs we send each other ... The important thing is to seem to be on the verge.[35]

In the fragmented company, which is subject to the whims of the stock market and the threat of outsourcing and in which there is no longer any possibility of having a career, what could be more natural than feeling you are "on the verge of a wonderful change"? What could be more attractive than the promise of a wonderful story?

The Destructuring Effects of the Apologia for Permanent Change

Looking down from the new Anglo-American heights of the new capital-ism, Richard Sennett reaches this conclusion: "The peculiar thing about the contemporary philosophy of capitalism is that disorder seems desir-able: the permanent restructuring of a firm is seen as a sign of its dynamism and, on the stock markets, institutional change has a value in its own right." These frenzied changes are not unrelated to the fact that capitalists now think in terms of a shorter time-span: "In 1960, the value of a company was evaluated on the basis of the profits it could be expected to make over a three-year period; on average, values are now calculated on a three-months basis."[36]

The new "post-Fordist" firm breaks the rules of the unity of time and place that governed the Fordist firm and scatters its workforce. Accord-ing to Sennett, the new capitalism has become "a system that is more neutral, and that promises less in social and psychological terms than the capitalism Max Weber analyzed one hundred years ago."[37] The psycho-technical synchronization of labor processes might be described as a piece of post-Fordist theater. But it is also a spatio-temporal synchroni-zation which ensured that the workforce perceived the temporal continuity that structured its life and work (a career and a working day, paid holidays, alternating periods of work and leisure, in-house train-ing). It created a feeling of being part of a collective endeavor, a company culture, or the great guild of the labor aristocracy. It may well have been illusory but it was also real, as was the feeling of being expropriated and exploited. The Fordist model therefore offered a stable model for pro-ductive synchronization and a certain unity of time and place (the factory and the working day). It defined what the Russian semiologist Mikhail Bakhtin called a "chronotope," or a spatio-temporal structure that was, in his view, a fundamental category of narrative structure.

It is this structuring story that has been destroyed by the apologia for permanent change. In an article on storytelling at the Renault car company, Olivier Blanquart, Pascale Malmaison, and Eddie Soulier write:

All organizations are immune systems and their goal, like that of any organism, is to preserve a certain status quo. But for the decision-makers, the adaptive value of change has becomes greater than that of stability. Mergers, restructurings, the development of technologies, internationalization, compulsory regulations and the implementation of new strategies are propelling the company into the spiral of change. Studies of change, however, confirm that individuals and organizations have an aversion for change.[38]

The deconstruction of the company's spatio-temporal identity has done much more to scramble workers' points of reference than the recruitment of peasants into the factories at the time of the Industrial Revolution: the general order to scatter will sound the death-knell for all "mobilizations," be they protest-based or productive, and the result will be absenteeism, a lack of motivation, and an increase in depressive symptoms amongst *cadres* (managers). The consultant Dominique Christian, who was one of the first in France to introduce storytelling, expresses this, not without a certain pathos, in a book entitled *Count, Recount? The Narrative Strategy*: "A sad cohort of regrets swirl around managers, like a swarm of bats. Remorse for what they have done to others: robbed them. Remorse for what they did not display towards others: solidarity. Remorse for what they are doing to others: exclusion and non-recognition. Remorse for what they are not doing with others: lost opportunities."[39]

A writer for the *New York Times* declares that "job apprehension has invaded everywhere, diluting self-worth, splintering families, fragmenting communities, altering the chemistry of workplaces."[40] Today, a young American with at least two years of college can expect to change jobs at least 11 times in the course of working, and change his or her skill base at least three times during those forty years of labor. The skills he or she will use at the age of forty will not be those he or she acquired at school. No one will spend their entire career with the same company: "Career jobs are dead," writes Yves-Frédéric Livian, professor at Lyon's Institut d'administration des enterprises. "Careers are no longer made inside companies: there is talk of 'post-corporate careers' ... But it is the notion of 'careers without frontiers' or 'nomadic careers' that will become the inescapable point of reference."[41]

Storytelling's Response

From 1995 onwards, far from encouraging writers on management to challenge the injunction to change and flexibility, this demobilization inspires them to make more and more proposals aimed at triggering a new emotional remobilization and a renewed commitment. "Hence the plethora of invitations to accept organizational change," write Blanquart, Malmaison, and Soulier,

> ranging from project-management methods to ways of persuading people to accept organizational change, as well as more psycho-sociological approaches. As well as these tactical approaches to change, we also have the company strategy known as the "learning company" model [which] demands the permanent regeneration of activities and the company itself ... takes the form of a need for quicker and more effective learning processes.[42]

"Two models are often invoked in the new career story," writes Yves-Frédéric Livian:

> The Hollywood movie milieu is often used as a benchmark in descriptions of a world in which individuals and companies collaborate because they can provide services for each other; they come together on a temporary basis to carry out a "project"-type task. Silicon Valley is also used as an illustration. Skills are developed within a dense network of companies, and migrate from company to company in a labor market that is both open and innovative.[43]

The "big bang" that Peter Drucker called for in the 1980s has exploded the Fordist paradigm. Capitalism's new ideology prefers change to continuity, mobility to stability, tension to equilibrium, and outlines a new organizational paradigm: a decentralized and nomadic company that recognizes no frontiers, that has been freed from laws and jobs, that is light, nimble, and furtive, and which acknowledges no law but the story it tells about itself, and no reality other than the fictions it sends out into the world.

"Lightness, quickness, exactitude, visibility, multiplicity, and consistency." That ought to be a good summary of new management's values. It is far from that. These are the titles of the six lectures the Italian writer Italo Calvino was meant to deliver in the United States in 1985–86. He chose what he saw as the six essential values that should be the twenty-first century's *episteme*. He wrote the first five, which were published posthumously as *Six Memos for the Next Millennium*.[44] Death prevented him from writing the sixth. The six values that were, in Calvino's view, the most valuable heritage of the novel are now central to the "storytelling management" project. All that remains of the sixth lecture is the title — "consistency"; we know that Calvino intended to discuss Herman Melville's novella *Bartleby, The Scrivener*, which has already been mentioned. It is subtitled: "A Story of Wall Street."

The success of storytelling from the 1990s onwards is a determinate response to the mutation organizations have experienced. The "network" structure of new companies increases the need for interaction. Collaboration between teams is replacing the old hierarchies, and the circulation of knowledge is replacing the narrow specialization of the assembly line. The autonomy of agents mirrors the outsourcing or automation of production. Getting a company to accept the ideology of change now presupposes that everyone becomes immersed in and surrenders to a shared fiction in the same way that we become wrapped up in a novel. It also presupposes that the company's culture takes the form of a story about *desired change*, and that forms of communication both inside and outside the company, modes of institutional cooperation, and forms of technological and social cooperation, all obey the transformational grammar of narrative.

Storytelling thus proves to be the best vector for the ideology of change, and the discursive form of the "mutant" organization. Management therefore tries to inspire in cadres and employees the attitude evoked by Jean Genet in a very different context. The "sudden departure" position (the position Indian women adopt as they squat on their heels, always ready to catch a child or perform some domestic task) implies a particular state of mind which consists, to cite Don DeLillo one last time, in the feeling of "being on the verge of a wonderful change."

4   The Mutant Companies of New-Age Capitalism

At the beginning of 2001, the director general of the auto company Renault Group's parts and accessories division (which designs, markets, and distributes Renault spares and accessories worldwide) began an experiment in storytelling when the division moved out of its premises. The project, code-named "e-DPA," was designed to take advantage of the removal in order to introduce new bureaucratic technologies and to infuse the whole division with a dynamic of change.

Managing Removals at Renault

"The study's objectives are clear," write the consultants who carried it out. "Our goal is not to audit the project, but to record the history of the project as it is experienced by a group of individuals [by concentrating on] the difficult moments in this adventure, not in order to challenge individuals, but to adopt the perspective of managerial capitalization and the logic of communications. The team scrupulously respects the anonymity of the interviewees."[1] The method used was inspired by one developed by MIT's Center for Organizational Learning, which has established seven successive stages for collecting and processing stories inside a company.

The first phase helps to identify learning processes, to define the target audience, the "perimeter of the capitalization of experiences," the questions that have to be asked, and the preconditions for management's involvement. The second phase involves collecting data from between ten and twenty people who are interviewed using ethnographic-style interviews; these are used to turn the lived experiences the company wants to describe into a narrative. The recorded interviews are transcribed in their entirety.

Stage 3, "Condensation and Distillation," gives an initial synthesis of the themes and plots that came up in the conversations, and produces a "coding plan" that allows all the stories to be merged into a coherent whole. The most interesting stories are organized thematically and put into a single time sequence. "The notion of distillation is carefully chosen," write the authors,

> to get across the essence of this activity, which consists in taking the huge volume of data that came out of the interviews, and then in correcting, filtering the raw data and refining it into a form that the organization can understand. The goal of the distillation process is to balance out three sets of data: the factual data that guarantees the story's credibility; the narrative data that makes the story human and interesting, in the form of vignettes, for example; and finally the messages, which must have a transformative effect on those they are addressed to.

Weekly meetings (stage 4) allowed almost 600 pages of transcript to be analyzed and reduced to 100 or so pages. The team chose 21 of the 100 little stories that had been selected, and used them to construct a final story of 22 pages. The story was written using the concept of the "jointly told tale," which is borrowed from ethnography: it is told both by the ethnographer, represented here by the storytelling team (which could just as well be made up of professional historians), and by his informants (actors from the company who had been directly involved in the story being told). The way it is written borrows the "two column format," which respects the polyphony of participants and observers. The story is then validated (stage 5) to check the chronology, quotations from the participants, and the initial interpretation. Finally, the story is distributed, first inside the company (stage 6) and then to a broader outside audience (stage 7), to ensure that the company projects a good image of managerial innovation. The authors conclude:

> This experiment confirms the importance of using this technique to analyse planned changes that have a rich human content. The project's actors can be described as "precursor heroes": they have left a place where they have worked for many years, have moved from private offices to open spaces, have reduced by a factor of ten the documents

they keep, have been introduced to technologies (NICTs), and have learned to book a meeting room on the Intranet, all within a very short space of time.

Computer-Assisted Storytelling

As this example demonstrates, the introduction of storytelling into a company follows very strict rules. It is not simply a matter of humanizing the management of "human resources," but of capturing workplace relations in a narrative net that takes the form of an oral story by submitting it to computerized writing and tracking, both at the level of collecting the stories, and that of processing, coding, and distributing them.

Storytelling makes it possible to collect expert stories, to identify the important stages in the decision-making process, and to identify the actors who played a role in the implementation of a project. It is, however, a cumbersome and expensive process. Hence the need to computerize the collection of narrative fragments, to encode stories so as to facilitate their use, and to systematize the way they are circulated. Storytelling is not a single flow that is fed by a supply of microstories collected from the teams, but rather a multiplicity of discursive centers that is structured by the way the stories are recorded and by the procedures used to retranscribe and redistribute them. The term also refers to the set of techniques that transform spontaneous stories into useful stories; as they are collected, the mechanisms used to record the stories combine spontaneous stories with "constrained" stories, and narration with prescription.

Postindustrial companies increasingly think of themselves as machines for *processing stories*. There are times and places for collecting stories: the water cooler, the elevator, the workshops at which stories are shared, the Internet, and the Intranet. Companies have their story banks, and an interest in archiving and codifying. Carefully managing their narrative capital, they collect the stories that tell their history, index them, project them outwards and store them in their employees' memories. They draw up trees of causes and events, encode behaviors, and investigate "tracked experiences."[2] They spread "good practice" and make "tacit knowledge" explicit.

Storytelling is therefore not a spontaneous or somewhat naïve exercise in non-directive listening. The stories that are collected are regarded as raw materials to be refined, pruned, and codified. Before they can be transformed into true experience vectors that can be easily circulated, they must be modelled and distributed in accordance with computerized procedures:

> Having optimized the data, information, and knowledge, companies are now trying to use information technologies to process their narrative information. Storytelling refers both to the sharing of narratives and to the methods and tools that are used to process the narrative information and facilitate its circulation inside the company so as to improve knowledge-sharing, bring together virtual communities, develop skills, decide, communicate or innovate.[3]

Research into narrative thus overlaps with research into information and communications science and technologies in order to develop new methods for modelling, simulation, and tests—and the appropriate software. How can computerized processing techniques be used to identify narrative elements that are formulated in spoken language? Is it possible to formalize, in machine-readable form, the information elements contained in narrative documents on, for example, relations between people and events?

These are the questions storytelling engineers tell themselves, and they are resolved to take seriously the possibility of computerizing stories. Narrative Knowledge Representation Language, for example, is a computer environment designed to process narrative documents. Some software packages, such as Hyperstoria, make it possible to break a narrative text down into segments, to label its main elements and arrange its propositions into a temporal-causal sequence, to identify scenes and to draw up trees of causes and decisions. Ontostoria, which was developed by Eddie Soulier in 2004, is designed to computerize the indexing of narratives and produce a narrative ontology based upon the principles of cognitive semantics using classes of terms (almost 150) predetermined by four main criteria (genre, plot, theme, and character). The expert selects those he or she finds pertinent to the indexing of the story.[4] "There is no doubt about it: the processing and communication of narrative data will cover ... most of the domains to which the ICTS are applied: multidimensional data, digitized documents, groupware, software, representations of knowledge, dialogue and interactivity, human learning and training environments, and so on."[5] Neo-management's eclectic enthusiasm for storytelling leads companies to think of themselves as narrative-performative spaces in which stories and tales replace or replicate internal regulations and time-clocks.

Given that the technostructure that once managed the technical synchronization of production can no longer handle these flows of information, computer-assisted storytelling appears to be the solution to many problems. It supposedly improves staff loyalty and commitment, orients and channels flows of information and the transmission of knowledge, allows experiences to be shared and incorporates qualitative, informal, and even subjective data. The in-house applications of storytelling go hand in hand with the trend to require everyone to talk about their lives and work, to transmit their skills, to mobilize their energies, and to accept change.

"Storytelling Companies"

Many studies carried out since the early 1980s have analyzed the crisis in big bureaucratic and hierarchical organizations and have demonstrated that the collapse of the Fordist model of post-war industrial capitalism has led to the emergence of a new model for a decentralized, flexible company that is structured into networks and focused on its core activity. This is an organization made up of autonomous agents who can take decisions and adapt to an uncertain environment. The new company is often likened to a project agency similar to a Hollywood production. It involves a mode of cooperation that is limited in both time and space, characterized by the performative logic of "one-offs" (or what marketing calls "experiences") and which excludes series, status, and careers.

This new generation of companies will be the figurehead of the new finance capitalism (euphemistically, but unscientifically, dubbed the "new economy"). These "mutant" companies represent capitalism's new age, which the American economist Jeremy Rifkin describes as "cultural" in *The Age of Access*.[6] They are usually characterized by their ultra-rapid growth (start-ups), their mastery of new technologies, their sector of activity (the tertiary sector, assuming that it includes pension funds and banks), and their reliance on "knowledge" character (to use what is already a dated conception of the knowledge economy), or "learning" to use a more recent concept of knowledge management.

Yet none of these categories allows us to understand the similarities between Apple and Starbucks, Enron and Nokia, Motorola and Google, Danone and Renault. And according to James B. Twitchell's *Branded Nation*, the list has to be extended to include some religious communities (such as the Willow Creek "megachurch"), great American universities such as Harvard, and even the Metropolitan Museum of Art and the Guggenheim Foundation.[7] Some management theorists, like David M. Boje describe them as "storytelling" organizations. "Every workplace, school, government office or local religious group is a *Storytelling Organization*. Every organization, from a simple office supply company or your local choral company, to the more glamorous entertainment organizations such as Disney or Nike, and the more scandalous such as Enron or Arthur Anderson, and even McDonald's are *Storytelling Organizations*."[8] In such organizations, stories are regarded both as a factor in innovation and change, a vector for learning, and a tool for communications. Storytelling is both a response to the crisis of meaning within organizations, and a method that can be used to construct a company identity. It structures and formats communications for both consumers and shareholders.

Storytelling is a more complex operation than it might seem at first sight. It is not simply a matter of telling employees' stories, or concealing reality behind a veil of deceptive fictions. It is also a matter of using a set of shared beliefs to encourage loyalty and to manage flows of emotion, or in other words of creating a constraining collective myth:

> Stories can be prisons ... In the family, we have certain roles to play, certain scripts that get acted out over and over again. Some stories are absolutely addictive and we get hooked on playing our characters and waiting for that climactic moment when we get to play our favorite scene. Stories and storytelling can become part of the panoptic gaze and the hegemony of power. What, then, is a story? And what does it mean "to follow" a story?[9]

We can now understand why narrative has become one of management's main concerns: no matter whether it is applied to the coordination of tasks, the interaction between technologies, the sharing of practices, or the encouragement of change, storytelling is assumed to be a way of policing behaviors and teaching people to accept the need for change. It is at once a marketing tool, a tool for personnel management that helps to mobilize (and not just motivate) managerial strata, a way of regulating social relations, of transmitting knowledge, of crystallizing a brand's image and of selling products. It is also a keeper of memory and a support for strategic projects, communications, and action, a vector for experience and innovation, a tool for training leaders and a school of obedience, a crucible for forging an identity and a catalyst for change.

The power of neocapitalism (and its symbolic violence), which is often misunderstood, no longer has to do solely with the synchronization of capital and labor, as has been the case ever since the Industrial Revolution; it consists in creating fictions that have the power to mobilize and involve "partners"—employees and clients, managers and shareholders—in premeditated scenarios. Assembly lines are replaced by narrative spirals. Control and discipline give way to what is supposed to be a shared collective story. Storytelling can therefore be defined as the set of technologies that organize this new productive "verbosity," which is replacing the silence of the old workshops and factories. Neocapitalism's ambition is no longer to accumulate material wealth but to saturate fields of symbolic production and exchange, both inside and outside the company. Once it has been adopted by one division in a company, storytelling invades the others: marketing, in-house communications, "human resources" management, leadership training, strategy, project management and, more surprisingly still, financial management.

Enron: A Fabulous Story From Wall Street

"It's a fabulous, fabulous story…" That is how Enron's CEO ended a TV advertisement for the company in the spring of 2001, just a few months before it went bankrupt in such spectacular fashion. Enron was at the time the seventh biggest company in the USA, with an estimated value of almost $70 billion. One of the finest flowers of the "new economy," its shares were a favorite with investors and financial analysts, and for six years running it was *Fortune* magazine's "most innovative company." The price of its shares had soared by 90 percent in 2000, when the Internet bubble burst. Shortly afterwards, its share price collapsed.[10]

According to Bethany McLean, the *Fortune* journalist who was the first to express doubts about the giant Enron's financial solidity, the company was in fact a house of cards. The fabulous story of Enron is probably the most illuminating example of how the capitalist company has been transformed into a phenomenon of shared belief. It reveals the paradoxes and dangers of corporate storytelling, which had one of its most phenomenal successes with Enron. It was followed by an unprecedented financial disaster. Enron saw its assets go from $10 million to $65 billion within a space of 16 years. It took it 24 days to go bankrupt. Twenty thousand employees lost their jobs; $2 billion in pension and retirement funds disappeared.

Although the management gurus were quick to use Enron as a counterexample when it went bankrupt, what led the company to be so out of touch with financial and accounting realities and to confuse reality and fiction to such an extent that its own executives were brainwashed has to be explained without resorting to legal (lies, fraud) or ethical (cynicism, greed) criteria. When the Enron executives went on trial in 2006, the experts could not understand their failure and explained the biggest American bankruptcy since the 1930s with banal talk of a financial panic.

This model company, which was, according to the experts, run by the best brains in the United States and which had planned the future of energy and electricity, is the most striking example one could hope to find of the "fictional companies" that made storytelling their raison d'être and Wall Street their theater of operations. Enron had become a veritable financial mirage that fostered illusions not only amongst its employees, who had a vested interest in its growth, but also amongst the biggest banks in the world and Wall Street's financial analysts, accountants, and shareholders.

"In the public eye, Enron's mission was nothing more than the cover story for a massive fraud. But what brought Enron down is something more complex—and more tragic … The story of Enron is a story of human weakness, of hubris and greed and rampant self-delusion."[11] It is the story of Ken Lay, a man from a poor family and the son of a preacher who, as a boy, dreamed of making a fortune. According to legend, that dream began when he was four or five. In the film adapted from McLean and Elkind's book, we see a photo of the young Ken Lay perched on a tractor and dreaming for the first time, we are told, of the world of commerce. As ambitious as he was brilliant, he studied economics and, as soon as he had graduated, went to Washington to "change all that."

We are in the 1980s, and Ronald Reagan is president. In the film, we see Reagan giving a speech that appears to have been written by or for

Ken Lay: "Government is not the solution to our problem. Government is the problem. The societies that have achieved the most spectacular broad-based economic progress in the shortest period of time are not the most tightly controlled, not necessarily the biggest in size or the wealthiest in natural resources. No, what unites them is their readiness to believe in the magic of the marketplace."[12] The man George W. Bush nicknamed "Kenny Boy" began one of the most fervent advocacies of deregulation in the energy markets and launched a crusade to "liberate businessmen." In 1985, he took advantage of the government's decision to float gas shares to found Enron. In 2000, Kenny Boy was one of the most generous contributors to George W. Bush's presidential campaign.

Ken Lay recruited Jeff Skilling as CEO. Skilling's idea was to distribute energy in a new way and to transform it into financial instruments that could be traded like shares. "He was the prophet," recalls a woman who worked with him. "He said forget about this pipeline stuff, you know, the state pipelines in the ground." Enron became a "stock market" for natural gas. Jeff Skilling had a very specific idea of what Reagan called the "magic of the marketplace." He was the magician. Before he took over as CEO, he laid down one condition: the accounts had to be based upon mark-to-market accounting and not historical values. Arthur Anderson's accountancy consultancy accepted his conditions. Mark-to-market accounting means that the balance sheet shows, not real profits, but the entire estimated value on the day the contract was signed, or in other words likely values and hypothetical returns. To the outside world — explains the only financial analyst to have expressed his scepticism (he was sacked as a result of the pressure brought to bear by Enron) — this meant that Enron's profits were what Enron said they were: "They were saying we are going to sell power from this power plant in ten years for so many dollars per kilowatt, and there was no way to prove that they could do it."[13]

Jeff Skilling's idea of accountancy was fictional. By freeing himself from historical values, he transformed accountancy into an enchanted world.

In a company film that was presumably meant for in-house communications, Jeff Skilling can be seen playing himself and parodying the method of valuing market prices: "We've really pulled out all the stops. Origination: we did $20 million last year; I think we can do $120 million. Trading: $10 million. We can do $64 million this year. This is the way we're going to move from mark to market to what I call HFV (hypothetical future value) accounting. If we do that, we can add a gazillion dollars to the bottom line." He then bursts out laughing.

David M. Boje, the American storytelling specialist who has already been cited so often here, notably with reference to Nike, obviously took an interest in this archetypal story. He and his colleagues studied the Enron saga at length in order to "examine how statistics in financial reports and executive metatheatric presentations were used to recommend Enron stock ... how professionals tell stories with numbers [and] show the important role the rhetorical construction of financial measures played in the Enron failure."[14]

Stories: The Financial Manager's Best Currency

The Enron affair is symptomatic of the close relationship between a capitalism that is obsessed with the quest for short-term profits and the recourse to the sirens of storytelling as a way of justifying its actions. The financialization of economies since the 1980s, which was triggered by the growth of pension funds and institutional investors, has produced what the radical American economist Bennett Harrison calls "impatient capital": investors adjust their investments in the very short term and evaluate the returns in terms of share prices rather than dividends.

"Whereas in 1965," notes Richard Sennett, "American pension funds held stock for an average of 46 months, by 2000 much in the portfolios of these institutional investors turned over on an average of 3.8 months."[15] At the same time, as Nigel Thrift explains: "Public relations became a crucial determinant of many aspects of economic life ... and increasingly, therefore, economic life came to resemble media industry with fashions, stars and favorite stocks."[16] The same point is made by Alicia Korten and Karen Dietz, who argue that "story is the new currency in financial management":

> In the world of finance, storytelling plays a vital role. "You won't get someone investing time and capital with just facts. It takes more than numbers if there's a decision on the table. Attracting investors is about being a good storyteller," says Dan Hendrix, president and CEO of Interface, Inc., the world's largest manufacturer of modular carpet and a leader in the sustainable business movement. Dorothea Brennan,

board member for Gaylord Hospital, a long-term acute care hospital, agrees: "Stories are vital for giving meaning to numbers. They provide context and capture people's imagination."[17]

During the 1990s, share prices broke free of companies' results, and the share price of companies that were not making a profit rose. "Enormous pressure was put on companies to look beautiful in the eyes of the passing voyeur; institutional beauty consisted in the demonstrating signs of internal change and flexibility, appearing to be a dynamic company."[18] It is not often that a prosperous company fires 10 percent of its employees every year. Enron's staff were ranked on a scale of one to five. Every year, 10 percent achieved the lowest score and were fired. Conversely, a twenty-five-year-old who was well-rated could come out of the CEO's office with a bonus of $5 million.[19]

The more the world of finance distanced itself from rational forecasts and economic success, the more the business cosmetics that makes companies look beautiful and desirable to investors became an important part of the management of these new organizations. Their "beauty" was in fact based upon the stories that told of restructuring, downsizing, and outsourcing.

The theme of Enron's last advertising campaign in 2001 was… market transparency. It was released a few weeks before the company went bankrupt; it showed traders in front of computer screens screaming "Buy" orders into their cell phones. A voiceover explains: "Enron Online… is creating an open transparent market that replaces the dark, blind system that existed beforehand." The film then cuts to a group of blind people wearing Disney masks, feeling their way with white sticks and assisted by guide-dogs.

In a rational world, this exemplary fiasco would have signalled the death of storytelling and its hypnotic values. And yet, almost ten years later, storytelling is—more so than ever—the management guru's bible. But it is also the bible of the spin doctors and "political gurus" who, with increasing success, have long been importing the methods of *storytelling management* into the United States (and many other countries).

5 Turning Politics Into a Story

"At the Faulkner household, it's known as 'The Hug.'" That makes it sound like a painting or sculpture, but it is in fact a photograph of young Ashley with the president of the United States. George W. Bush is shown full face, hugging a fifteen-year-old girl. The photograph was taken by her father, marketing consultant Lynn Faulkner, on May 6, 2004, at a rally in Lebanon, Ohio, during the presidential election campaign. Sent by e-mail to a few family friends, it began to circulate amongst Bush supporters on the Internet. And within a few days, it had been seen all over the United States. "'People can immediately see in that photo an authenticness,' Lynn Faulkner said. 'I think that's why the image continues to travel.'"[1]

Ashley's Story

A few weeks later, the conservative lobby Progress for America Voter Fund suggested to Lynn Faulkner that Ashley's story should be turned into a campaign advertisement. He agreed. "The Hug" became *Ashley's Story*, a commercial that was shown 30,000 times on local TV channels in the nine swing states where the outcome of the clash between Republicans and Democrats was uncertain. According to observers on both sides, it changed the course of the presidential election of November 2004.[2] "Karl Rove and his team of Republican operatives are accepting congratulations for engineering President Bush's re-election campaign. But there's another less likely Republican who deserves a lot of credit for the president's win: Lebanon, Ohio resident Lynn Faulkner."[3]

"My wife Wendy was murdered by terrorists on 11 September..." That is how *Ashley's Story* begins. The man who is speaking to the camera is standing in front of the family bookcase in his shirt sleeves. His name appears at the bottom of the screen: Lynn Faulkner, Mason, Ohio. The camera zooms in on a photo of his wife and her two daughters, who are about ten. The voiceover goes on: "After her mother's death, the Faulkners' daughter Ashley had closed up emotionally." On the screen, a photo shows Ashley sprawled in a hammock and reading a classic novel with a portrait of a woman in Victorian dress on the cover. The voiceover goes on: "But when President George W. Bush came to Lebanon, Ashley went to see him, just as she did with her mother four years earlier."

The music moves from a minor to a major key and speeds up as we see images of Bush shaking hands with people in the crowd. Linda Prince, a friend of the Faulkners who attended the rally with Ashley describes what happened next: "As the President approached, I said to him: 'Mr. President, this young lady lost her mother in the World Trade Center.'"

"He turned towards me," says Ashley Faulkner, who was filmed a few weeks later in the garden of the family home. "He said to me: 'I know it's hard. Are you OK?'"

Linda Prince: "Our president took Ashley in his arms and hugged her to his chest [the camera shows the photo of Ashley in Bush's arms]. And it was at that moment, we saw Ashley's eyes fill up with tears."

Ashley Faulkner: "He's the most powerful man in the world, and all he wants to do is make sure I'm safe, that I'm OK."

Lynn Faulkner, the girl's father, then concludes: "What I saw was [shot of newspaper headline: "Bush comforts daughter of 9/11 victim"] what I wanted to see in the heart [shot of Bush congratulating a firefighter at Ground Zero] and soul of the man who sits in the highest elected office in the land." The commercial ends with a shot of George W. Bush in profile, eyes downcast and in a contemplative mood. The music ends on a major chord.[4]

A 9/11 Family

It was the most expensive commercial of the 2004 presidential election campaign, costing $6.5 million according to a study from the Center for Public Integrity. Television broadcasts during the last three weeks of the campaign were backed up by a communications exercise that involved sending out over 2.3 million brochures, the sending millions of e-mails, and an automated telephone campaign.[5] Its success was without precedent in the history of American political campaigns, and

Ashley's Story has become an object of study for communications researchers.

According to the University of Maryland's Susan Allen: "The ad has earned praise for its effectiveness from analysts on both sides."[6]

"It was a very effective piece of political advertising because it was a personal story," says John Green, a political scientist at the University of Akron in Ohio, a state that, not surprisingly, was inundated with campaign spots this year. "It took a grand, ugly thing [terrorism] and put it in a context people can understand. That picture of Bush with the little girl is very effective television ... The ad breaks one taboo in using a motherless child to deliver one part of the ad's message, but few charges of exploitation have been leveled against the ad, in part because Ashley's father delivers the message in a low-key, non-combative tone."[7]

According to *Salon* web magazine, *Ashley's Story* had an impact because it was "memorable, motivating, and feel-good."[8] The commercial only lasts for 60 seconds, but it is indeed remarkably effective: a rapid montage of a sequence of brief shots showing the various eye-witnesses reinforces the coherence and credibility of the story. Although he is the central figure in the narrative, the president does not say anything. He is neither expressing an idea nor outlining a program. He is all serenity and kindness. Although he has helped to work a sort of miracle, he is present only through the eye-witness accounts that describe his actions and words, as in the life of a saint in the Gospel story.

Young Ashley first appears in photographs (first with her mother and sister, and then reading in the hammock), but she is the one who delivers the key message: "He's the most powerful man in the world, and all he wants to do is make sure I'm safe, that I'm OK." Linda Prince, the family friend who stands in for the girls' absent mother and who introduced Ashley to the president, plays an essential part. She confirms that the girl underwent an emotional transformation: a "psychological recovery," with Bush as its medium: "And it was at that moment that we saw Ashley's eyes fill up with tears."

The president's intervention brings her out of her emotional "closure." His compassion has a healing effect: "When [Bush] wrapped his arms around her and pulled her to his chest, she really did show more feeling and more pain than she had in the past three years. She said it was the first time she had felt safe since her mother's murder."[9] Ashley's father, who took the photo, plays the role of the eye-witness. He opens and closes the story, but without completely destroying its mystery. He describes his meeting with Bush as though he were describing a supernatural phenomenon: "What I saw was what I want to see in the heart and soul of the man who sits in the highest elected office in our country."

The photo-memory of the mother with her two daughters, the images of Bush mingling with crowd, the reproduction of the local paper that reported the event during which the president comforted the daughter of a 9/11 victim, and the photo of Bush congratulating a New York firefighter are all exhibits that confirm the accuracy of what is being reported and confirm the ad's central message, delivered by the girl.

Sociologist Francesca Polletta emphasizes the great importance of the word *safe* — "Are you all right?" It means free from danger or injury, but it also has a therapeutic meaning: "It represented the 9/11 attack as something that was experienced by those in America's heartland, and represented its victims as Bush supporters ... The spot also turned the terrorist threat into something that had taken place in the past. Making Ashley safe meant easing the emotional after-effects of a terrorist attack, not protecting her from future attack."[10]

The Faulkners were quite right: the photo of Ashley in Bush's arms does look like a holy picture or an icon of compassionate conservatism. Ashley's story borrows its narrative codes from a biblical parable: it is the story of an important event, namely a memorable encounter followed by a miracle cure. At the end of the commercial we see Bush congratulating a New York firefighter; the photo has been subtly retouched to present the figure of the president in a stance and a light that evoke pictures of Christ and the saints.

"They Produce a Narrative, We Produce a Litany"

Ashley's Story is a masterpiece of manipulation. It can be seen as storytelling's sanctioning — and revision — of a job description that emerged 20 years earlier in the world of American politics: "communications adviser" or "spin doctor." The term "spin," which was coined by Ronald Reagan's adviser in 1984, was first used during a televised debate with Democratic candidate Walter Mondale. Although Mondale far outclassed the outgoing president, Reagan's aide Lee Atwater said after the debate: "Now we're going to go out here and spin this afterward."[11] "Afterward" was a reference to the "debate about the debate," which is now as important a part of a presidential campaign as the debate itself. Thanks to an intense "spinning" campaign, it allowed Reagan to win the debate.

Lee Atwater, who died in 1991, was the perfect example of the shadowy advisers journalist Jack Rosenthal dubbed "spin doctors" in an op-ed piece in the *New York Times* on October 21, 1984, the day of the debate itself. The term was inspired by the "spin" that is applied to a tennis or billiard ball, or the way a top spins. Spin doctors can therefore be defined as "influencing" agents who supply arguments, images, and stage directions that have the desired effect on public opinion.

After the Democrats lost the 2004 election, James Carville, one of the spin doctors who had engineered Bill Clinton's victory in 1992, stated: "I think we could elect someone from the Hollywood Hills if they had a narrative to tell people about what the country is and where they see it." Republican pollster Stanley Greenberg told reporters: "A narrative is the key to everything." A few days later on *Meet the Press*, Carville was even more explicit: "They produce a narrative, we produce a litany. They say, 'I'm going to protect you from the terrorists in Tehran and the homos in Hollywood.' We say, 'We're for clean air, better schools, more health care.'"[12]

Is saying "I'll protect you from the terrorists in Tehran and the homos in Hollywood" really a narrative? Probably not, if we are thinking in terms of purely literary categories. But using the phrase in the context of an election did indeed have the effect of plunging Republican voters into a narrative world. According to Francesca Polletta, what Carville was actually saying was: "The Republicans gave voters villains and heroes; new characters in age-old dramas of threat, vengeance, and salvation. The Democrats ticked off a dry list of familiar issues."[13] According to Carville, the Republicans had succeeded in presenting the election issue in the form of a plot that could easily be understood and that could mobilize simple emotions like fear, loneliness, and the need for protection. They invited on to the political stage sympathetic heroes (middle-class Americans) and villains (the terrorists in Tehran and the homos in Hollywood) and created a narrative tension between them. The election of the Republican candidate would, it was implied, resolve that tension.

Paul Begala, another Democrat spin doctor, described how John Kerry consulted him in 2004, at a time when he was doing badly in the polls. Knowing that Kerry was a former prosecutor, he advised him to defend his candidacy before voters as though he were pleading a case in court. According to his notes, Kerry came up with a list of six key themes: jobs, taxes, fiscal policy, health care, energy, and education. "This was a list, not a 'case,'" Begala fretted.[14] "If you are not communicating in stories," write Carville and Begala, "you're not communicating. That's why, from the Greek myths to the griots of Africa, the history of humanity has been told in stories." In their view, the art of telling stories is one of the 12 secrets that make it possible to win an election: "Facts tell, but stories sell."[15]

The celebrated marketing guru Seth Godin's analysis is the same: "Why did John Kerry lose against an incumbent with near-record-low approval ratings after spending more than $100,000,000 on his campaign? Simple. He didn't tell a coherent story, a lie worth remembering, a story worth sharing ... Like him or not, George W. Bush did an extraordinary job of living the story of the strong, certain, infallible leader. John Kerry tried to win on intellect and he lost because too few voters chose to believe a story they perceived as inconsistent and unclear."[16]

Interviewed by *Newsweek* in October 2006, mid-way through the midterm elections, James Carville again contrasted the Republican narrative with the Democrat litany. Asked why Democrats were having so much trouble getting elected, he replied:

Because the Democrats have a predictable litany. "I believe in a woman's right to choose. I believe a good school system is essential to what we are. I stand for the minimum wage." Blah, blah, blah. It's like when I was an altar boy: "I believe in the virgin birth, I believe in this and that." The [real] narrative (of the Christian litany) is "We were a bunch of sinners and Jesus came and died and bled and saved us all." As John Kerry was going through this predictable litany during the [2004 presidential] election, Bush was out there saying, "I was a drunk and I was saved by the power of Jesus Christ and I was saved by 9/11, and I will protect you from the terrorists in Tehran and the homos in Hollywood." It's a narrative voters can relate to. The Democrats' first inclination is to expand the litany, rather than developing a focused narrative. Most elements of the litany I'm fine with. But we're not going to win by reciting it.[17]

A few weeks before the 2004 election, William Safire, an old hand at political communications, mocked the spin doctors' explanations in an article entitled "The Way We Live Now." Mocking their analysis ("gotta have a plot—no plot, no narrative coherence"), he cites one of their number as saying that if they had won, the "Democrats would have been congratulating the Kerry campaign for having constructed a coherent narrative." "After an event, there are people who want to control the perception of that event, and the way they do that is by intervening with a narrative." The Democrat's post-election "narrative" was that "Kerry had no coherent narrative."

William Safire cites the analysis of Peter Brooks, an academic specialist in the theory of narrative: "The use of the word narrative is completely out of hand! ... While I think the term has been trivialized through overuse, I believe the over-use corresponds to a recognition that narrative is one of the principal ways in which we organize our experience of the world—a part of our cognitive tool kit that was long neglected by psychologists and philosophers."[18]

Prosecutor Starr, who wrote the report on the Monica Lewinsky affair, presented his major findings in a section titled "Narrative," "in a play for public acceptance" of his interpretation. Safire cites Peter Brooks as saying: "Had Starr chosen a more cubist approach, readers would of course have constructed their own narratives ... The claim that there was one narrative was a pre-emptive strike against dissenting opinions. (In the same way, Lee Hamilton of the 9/11 commission said of its 2004 report: 'We finally cut all adjectives and ended up with a sparse narrative style.')"[19] The suggestion that there was only one possible narrative presumably improved the book's sales.

William Safire was mocking those he called the "politerati" (literate politicians) and the "narratological" vulgate the spin doctors seized upon in the American success of the structural analysis of narrative inaugurated by Roland Barthes, Gérard Genette, Algirdas Greimas, and a few others. It paved the way for the new discipline Tzvetan Todorov called "narratology," or the science of narrative. Barthes' idea that narrative is one of the great cognitive categories that allows us to understand and organize the world was developed in Paris within a small circle of researchers at the Ecole des Hautes Etudes. It had enjoyed such success in the United States that it was becoming something that any fool studying political science was familiar with. This was probably the first time that the name of Roland Barthes had appeared in a *New York Times* op-ed piece on an American election, but it demonstrates the extent to which political science had adopted the language and concepts of the literary criticism of the 1960s.

Yet when President Bush's popularity rating collapsed after Hurricane Katrina in August 2005, the same Safire rallied in despair to the narrative approach he had mocked in his December 2004 article. "I think now we're in the grip of a narrative. And the narrative is 'The president and this presidency is finished.' And his polls are way down. He didn't do Katrina right, the war is not over. And everything he does is shaded by this narrative." Safire had not, however, lost hope: the situation might still turn in favor of Bush, not because of some resolute action on behalf of New Orleans and its population, but simply because the media coverage required it to do so: "The wonderful thing about American attention and media coverage, is the narrative has to change. It can't stay the same, or else it's not newsworthy. And so the story will be the comeback."[20]

Power Through Narrative

Why does storytelling have such a grip on political discourse in the United States? Why is telling edifying stories seen as a new paradigm for the political sciences, and why has it replaced the notions of images and rhetoric to such an extent that it dominates not only election campaigns, but also the exercise of executive power and the management of crisis situations? American political scientists usually invoke three kinds of reasons: the first is the national fiber of Americans; the second refers to the talent of individuals and especially of Ronald Reagan, who was proclaimed by Carville and Begala to be "the greatest storyteller to grace the White House in the last fifty years."[21] The third evokes the "spirit of the times," which is described as "postmodern," and in which, now that the grand narratives have collapsed, the emphasis is on anecdotes and the appeal of short stories illustrating the ferocious competition between values and legitimation-vectors.

As we have seen, Evan Cornog, who teaches journalism at Columbia and was cited in the introduction, opts for the first explanation: "The essence of American presidential leadership, and the secret of presidential success, is storytelling."[22] According to Cornog, all American presidential candidates share a common history of American myths and heroes, and must inscribe themselves in that narrative lineage by using their family background and personal history and comparing it with that of other candidates during presidential campaigns: "It is the battle of stories, not the debate on issues, that determines how Americans respond to a presidential contender."[23] For Cornog, "These crafted narratives are the principal medium of exchange of our public life, the currency of American politics."[24] Not one to be afraid of grandiloquence, he boldly concludes that: "The future of the nation, and of the world, depends upon the abilities of American citizens to choose the right stories."[25]

It is undeniable that the lives and political histories of American presidents were turned into "stories" and even heroicized long ago. That may, however, have more to do with Hollywood's role in American society than with some presidential "essence." And, even if it were a matter of a presidential "essence," the fact remains that the stories that grew up around the figure of, for example, Lincoln,[26] have nothing to do with the use the story spinners have made of them since the 1990s. Some tell their stories *a posteriori*, in order to legitimize presidential actions or to turn them into legend, while others manufacture stories in order to win and then exercise power, and control their viral distribution in order to create the horizon of expectations that will give them consistency, and manipulate the socio-technical conditions for their distribution and interpretation. In a word, they establish the concrete preconditions for their dissemination throughout society.[27]

There is also a danger that any attempt to explain the triumph of political storytelling in terms of the American "national character" will obscure the historical and transdisciplinary nature of the narrative turn; from the mid 1990s onwards, it affected domains as diverse as management, marketing, politics, and the defense of the nation. The "genetic" explanation in fact generates clichés about the American "political spectacle" and suggests that political storytelling has simply replaced the old marketing, with its parades of majorettes, ticker tape, and giant neon signs.

Historians of the presidency such as Jeffrey K. Tulis, in contrast, point out that, received wisdom notwithstanding, the founding fathers were suspicious of clever speeches because they "manifest demagogy,

impede deliberation, and subvert the routine of republican government."
The founding fathers feared the dangers of what we now call the democracy of public opinion or direct democracy; they wanted to ensure that
political decisions would not be swayed by shifts in public opinion.
Deliberative government, indirect elections, the principle of the separa-
tion of powers, and the independence of the executive were all designed
to ward off the threat of manipulation. "The now commonplace practice
of direct public appeals was shunned during the nineteenth century
because it went against existing interpretations of the constitutional
order."[28]

The usual reason for rejecting the first hypothesis—that storytelling is
a permanent feature of American presidencies or the essence of presidential power—is the alternative hypothesis that Ronald Reagan introduced
a new governance, a sort of "narratocracy" or narrative presidency. "Our
political leaders' love of stories may no doubt have less to do with
Barthes and his followers than with Ronald Reagan, who, I believe, was
the first US president to govern largely by anecdote."[29] There are serious
arguments to support this thesis, and it is true that the presidents who
followed Reagan into the White House used his method of communication, imitating and sometimes even plagiarizing his speeches.

The journalist Serge Halimi looks, for example, at two State of the
Union Addresses.[30] The first is by Ronald Reagan (February 6, 1985)
and the second by George W. Bush (January 23, 2007). There are a lot
of similarities between them—the occasion, the authority that legiti-
mates them, and the discursive style which makes them so similar that
one might think they were written by the same person.

Ronald Reagan:

Two hundred years of American history should have taught us that
nothing is impossible. Ten years ago a young girl left Vietnam with her
family, part of the exodus that followed the fall of Saigon. They came
to the United States with no possessions and not knowing a word of
English. Ten years ago—the young girl studied hard, learned English,
and finished high school in the top of her class. And this May, May
22nd to be exact, is a big date on her calendar. Just ten years from
the time she left Vietnam, she will graduate from the United States
Military Academy at West Point. I thought you might like to meet an
American hero named Jean Nguyen. [The "American" hero stands

and receives an ovation; Reagan tells another edifying story, and then reveals the moral of both stories.] Your lives tell us that the oldest American saying is new again. Anything is possible in America if we have the faith, the will, and the heart. History is asking us once again to be a force for good in the world.[31]

Twenty-two years later, George W. Bush entered the White House:

The greatest strength we have is the heroic kindness, courage, and self-sacrifice of the American people. You see this spirit often if you know where to look—and tonight we need only look above to the gallery. Dikembe Mutombo grew up in Africa, amid great poverty and disease. He came to Georgetown University to study medicine—but Coach John Thompson got a look at Dikembe and had a different idea. Dikembe became a star in the NBA, and a citizen of the United States, but he never forgot about the land of his birth—or the duty to share his blessings with others. He has built a brand new hospital in his hometown. A friend has said of this good-hearted man, "Mutombo believes that God has given him this opportunity to do great things." And we are proud to call this son of the Congo our fellow American.[32]

Bush goes on to tell other stories, like that of Julie Aigner-Clark who, after the birth of her daughter, founded the Baby Einstein Company, which makes educational videos for young children. In just five years, her company grew into a $200 million business, and she then went on to produce child-safety videos. "We are pleased to welcome this talented business entrepreneur and generous social entrepreneur—Julie Aigner-Clark." Then there was the story of Wesley Autrey, who was waiting at a Harlem subway station with his two little girls when he saw a man fall into the path of a train. "Wesley jumped on to the tracks ... pulled the man into a space between the rails ... and held him as the train passed right over their heads ... There is something wonderful about a country that produces a brave and humble man like Wesley Autrey." And finally, he told the story of Tommy Rieman, a young man from Independence, Ohio, who enlisted in the US Army. He was wounded in Iraq and awarded the Silver Star: "And like so many other Americans who have volunteered to defend us, he has earned the respect and gratitude of our whole country."

The moral of the stories is: "In such courage and compassion, ladies and gentlemen, we see the spirit and character of America—and these qualities are not in short supply."

The Great Communicator Reagan, and his Disciples Clinton and Sarkozy

As just noted, according to James Carville and Paul Begala, Ronald Reagan was "the greatest storyteller to have graced the White House in the last fifty years," even though many of his stories were simply false. In order to fan America's resentment against welfare, he told the story of "the welfare queen who'd purchased a Cadillac with government largesse." The facts were, of course, all wrong, but the point was clear: "hardworking Americans were the heroes, the welfare queen was the villain and the poor, beleaguered middle-class taxpayers were the victims. Reagan could simply have read a laundry list of statistics, but he knew a story would have an immeasurably greater impact."[33] "Reagan understood," writes Peter Brooks, "that the concrete particularity of storytelling will always be more vivid than compilations of facts."[34] Under Reagan's presidency, official discourse made more use of colorful stories that spoke to Americans' hearts rather than their intellect, and to their emotions rather than their opinions. Anecdotes replaced statistics in official speeches. And the president's inventions replaced reality. He sometimes evoked episodes from old war movies as though they were part of the real history of the United States.

And his successors remembered the lesson. A few weeks after his election, Bill Clinton surprised everyone by appointing David R. Gergen as his director of communications. Gergen had held that position under Reagan. On the day he took up his appointment, Gergen states: "They simply understood what Reagan had understood."[35] Twelve years later, Clinton confirmed this in his own way: "My Uncle Buddy taught me that everyone has a story."[36] He ends his autobiography with the words: "As I said, I think it's a good story."[37]

Throughout the 1,000 pages of a book that is full of anecdotes of uneven interest, Clinton constantly puts the history of America on the same plane as the story of a kid from Hope, Arkansas, who was born under a good star, and carefully considered decisions (which led to wars) on the same plane as ill-considered decisions that left stains on the dress of a White House intern. His marathon book is littered with all sorts of incidents, some fortuitous and some historic, family and international incidents, chance and planned encounters, and portraits of the celebrities of the political world as well as unknowns. It is like reading an ad man's tribute to the American heartlands. History is stripped of any grandeur or epic profundity. The trouble with Clinton, who was described by an American comedian as "a tax and spin president," was that "he spins when the truth would serve him better. But once spin control becomes common it soon becomes a habit and then a way of life."[38]

In his memoirs, Clinton defends a novel conception of politics. In his view, politics no longer means solving economic, political, or military problems; *it must give people the opportunity to improve their stories*. Presidential power is no longer the power to take decisions or to organize things; the president is a screenwriter and director, and the main actor in a political sequence that lasts for the duration of his mandate, rather like TV series that grip everyone, such as *24* or *The West Wing*.

The White House, with the Oval Office at its heart, is viewed as a stage or the set where a film about the presidency is being shot. The "story" of a presidential candidate is a fiction that organizes a tangle of contradictory ideas, impressions, and actions, and makes them instantly comprehensible. The point is not to use a story to shed light on a lived experience, but simply to dress up silhouettes and bring them to life, to turn the new president and his entourage into characters in a "coherent story," and to popularize the saga of his doings. As Seth Godin puts it: "From the clothes he wears, to his spouse and his appointees, he's telling a story."[39]

Executive power becomes the power to "execute," to direct (in the cinematographic sense) a presidential screenplay that is viewed as a sequence of decisions that is constantly being edited. The highly symbolic activity of power boils down to this: the coordination of flows of information, centralized control over information policy, the power to influence the media, either directly or indirectly, and to mobilize support for the president's initiatives. That was precisely the program implemented by Nicolas Sarkozy, who was elected president of France in May 2007, during his election campaign and the first months of his presidency.

The dangers inherent in this use of power are obvious; as John Anthony Maltese put it in 1994: "A less deliberative process in government and the citizenry inundated with the symbolic spectacle of politics but ill-equipped to judge its leaders or the merits of their policies."[40] And according to Richard Rose in his book *The Postmodern President*: "A key to presidential power, then, is the ability to harness (or manufacture) opinion. The result is a sort of unending political campaign."[41]

Postmodern Presidents

In his inaugural lecture to the Collège de France on December 2, 1970, Michel Foucault told an anecdote about the Shogun of Japan:

> The Shogun had heard tell that the Europeans' superiority in matters of navigation, commerce, politics, and military skill was due to their knowledge of mathematics. As he had been told of an English sailor who possessed the secret of these miraculous discourses, he summoned him to his palace and kept him there. Alone with him, he took lessons. He learned mathematics. He retained power, and lived to a great age. It was not until the nineteenth century that there were Japanese mathematicians.
>
> This anecdote, so beautiful that one trembles at the thought that it might be true ... gathers into a single figure all the constraints of discourse: those which limit its powers, those which master its aleatory appearances, those which carry out the selections among speaking subjects.[42]

Is such an illusion still possible, now that the explosion of sources, forms, and producers of utterances has given rise to the proliferation of enigmatic signs that Jean-François Lyotard defines as "the postmodern condition"? How can we control the explosion of discursive practices on the Internet? How can we communicate in this chaos of fragmented knowledge without the help of some shared legitimizing figure? How can we ascribe a meaning to social and workplace experiences that are characterized by their precariousness and lack of any long-term future? How are we to establish sets, or a logical or chronological sequence? How are we to describe the conflicts of interest, the ideological or religious collisions, or the culture wars? These are some of the questions that have to be dealt with by public speech and all those who are responsible for its expression, be they journalists or politicians, advisers to the prince, specialists in political marketing or speech writers. This is why storytelling has become the "magic" formula that can inspire trust and even belief in voter-subjects.

Today's Shogun, or his heirs — the president of the Republic, the head of the general staff, or the spin doctors — would not burden themselves with a sailor-mathematician. They would set their heart on having a creole *conteur*, an African griot or, failing that, a storyteller. The post-modern paradigm is usually invoked to explain the downward spiral of political discourse. It could even be described as the spontaneous ideology of the new galaxy that the Internet has created. Like some new and expanding discursive universe, it is replacing the Gutenberg galaxy, and its unknown constellations are populated by millions of nameless stars, author-satellites, and black holes.

The chaos of fragmented knowledge facilitated the "narrative turn" in political communications and the advent of a new era. This is democracy's performative age, and its figureheads are no longer the advisers to the prince or the Talleyrands and the Mazarins, but the prophets, the gurus, and the parties; spin doctors, and their ability to tell stories and to mystify, has made them drunk. Storytelling is their *modus operandi* because it is the only thing that can get a hold on these dispersed interests and discourses. Never before has there been such a trend to view political life as a deceptive narrative designed to replace deliberative assemblies of citizens with a captive audience, while mimicking a sociability in which TV series, authors, and actors are the only things they are all familiar with. Its function is to create a virtual and fictional community. The trend is so astonishingly fluid, so much part of the spirit of the times, and so much part of the air we breathe and the general climate of the age, that it goes unnoticed. And that of course is the key to its irresistible success.

Watergate and the Coming of the Spin Doctors

If we wish to understand the "narrative turn" taken by American politics during the Reagan years, we have to go back to Nixon's presidency and the trauma of Watergate. It is impossible to understand Watergate without making an analysis of the concrete conditions (which are at once ideological and technical, political and institutional) that, in the 40 years between Nixon and George W. Bush, led to the general "fictionalization" of American political discourse (and its equivalents elsewhere in the West).

As soon as he took office, Richard Nixon declared that the press was the "enemy." Embittered by the treatment reserved for John F. Kennedy, the former political rival who became a legend when he was assassinated, and by the media dominance of liberals opposed to the war in Vietnam, Nixon urged his advisers (who already included Safire and Gergen) to bypass the Washington press. The beginnings of mass television worked to the advantage of his strategy of appealing directly to the American people and going over the heads of journalists. Bypassing the press and making direct appeals to the silent majority: both these characteristic features of the conservative revolution had already been clearly defined by Nixon.

Nixon's two mandates were the theater of a real war between the president and the media. Everyone remembers the final battle over Watergate, which ended with the president's resignation and the recognition that the press was the "fourth power"; but, while Watergate did usher in a new era, it was not that of journalistic counter-power. On the contrary, it ushered in the age of the hegemonic power of the spin doctors. That is obvious to anyone who reads John Anthony Maltese's *Spin Control* (1994), which reconstructs the history of the White House's "Office of Communications."

It was Nixon who established the Office of Communications. His reasons for doing so were simple, as the former president explains clearly in his memoirs: "[Modern presidents] must try to master the art of manipulating the media, not only in order to win in politics, but in order to further the programs and causes they believe in; at the same time, they must avoid at all cost the charge of trying to manipulate the media. Concern for image must rank with concern for substance."[43]

The growing number of media, the rise in the number of accredited journalists and the internationalization of media coverage eroded the intimate relationship between the government and the press that made it possible to restrict flows of information to only a few channels. Television gave direct access to the public and the development of satellites extended its range to the whole country and even internationally. Political power was increasingly subject to public opinion, and addressed it directly. Communication came to mean influencing public opinion rather than just feeding news to the press. Nixon called this "going public."

Looking back at his experience as President Gerald R. Ford's chief of staff, Dick Cheney (who was to become George W. Bush's vice-president) said precisely that, when in 1992 he admitted to John Anthony Maltese: "To have an effective presidency, the White House must control the agenda ... The most powerful tool you have is the ability to use the symbolic aspects of presidency to promote your goals and objectives. You don't let the press set the agenda ... They like to decide what's important and what isn't important. But if you let them do that, they're going to trash your presidency."[44] In those few lines, Dick Cheney defined the role of the White House Office of Communications. Its mission and organization remained the same from Nixon to Bush, despite all the handovers of power and political ups and downs.

The continuity is easily explained. The Office was staffed by a small group of men who took over from one another as power changed hands and who shaped a doctrine of political communications: Dick Cheney, James A. Baker III, David R. Gergen, Michael Deaver, Patrick Buchanan, William Safire, and a few others. Frank Ursomarso, who became Reagan's director of communications in February 1981, had already worked in the White House during the Nixon and Ford presidencies. David R. Gergen, who had been director of communications under Nixon, ran the office for Gerald Ford and then Ronald Reagan before being reappointed, as we have already seen, by Bill Clinton in 1992. Most of these men had lived through the trauma of Watergate, which put an end to the career of Richard Nixon. As Gergen explained to columnist Mark Hersgaard: "All of us came out of the Watergate years. I know a lot of people who went to jail, people whose careers crashed, people who were at the top who went to the bottom."[45]

After the chain of disasters of Nixon's forced resignation followed by the electoral defeats of Gerald Ford and Jimmy Carter—with the media playing a destabilizing role—Ronald Reagan entered the White House with a stubborn determination to control the press. His program was clear, and it called for a conservative revolution that would base its values upon public opinion. The appeal to the concept of "the silent majority" erupted into American political life. The technological revolution would allow it to penetrate the whole of the United States in real time.

Creating a Counter-Reality

The White House Office of Communications was given the responsibility of handling the presidency's strategic agenda. Its goal was to ensure that every member of the presidential team adhered to it and promoted it in public opinion by using a form of mass marketing. Every day a "line of the day" (in the 1990s, this became the "story of the day") was drawn up and distributed to the various branches of the executive and the accredited press, and also through televised messages addressed directly to the public. Focus groups and polls were used to elaborate presidential messages and sound-bites were inserted into the president's speeches in order to get them across, while his public appearances were stage-managed in order to reinforce their visual impact and block other messages.

The former Hollywood actor knew how to "follow the script," as Maltese puts is, but he was also helped by a team of communicators who knew how to "set the stage." It was headed by James Baker III, who had worked on Gerald Ford's campaign in 1976, and David R. Gergen, who had been Ford's director of communications: "We think we have the best communicator president since John Kennedy. We want to use him properly." It was Gergen who introduced the "line of the day." Developed during the Nixon presidency, the practice consisted in defining a daily presidential screenplay that was "sold" to the press. If journalists tried to depart from it, they were promptly pulled back into line. As President Reagan said one day: "If I answer that question now, none of you will say anything about what you're here for today. I'm not going to give you a different line."[46]

Ronald Reagan's talents are not in dispute, but they would have been useless without the Office of Communications' centralized control of the news or what the *New York Times* journalist Steven Weisman called "the art of control access": "The Reagan White House controlled the agenda, kept up the offensive, deflected criticism from the president, made sure the administration spoke with one voice, and molded its communications strategy around its legislative strategy." Under Reagan, the Office of Communications "helped to create a counter-reality through his visuals. The idea was to divert people's attention away from the substantive issues by creating a world of myths and symbols that made people feel good about themselves and their country."[47]

Thanks to Reagan and Clinton, political communications acquired new masters and adopted a new register—and this tendency would become even more pronounced with Bush and after 9/11. The goal was no longer simply to keep the public well-informed about the executive's decisions by trying to control the political agenda, but to create a virtual new world, an enchanted kingdom populated by heroes and anti-heroes that the citizen-actor was invited to enter. The point was now not so much to communicate as to create a story and force it on to the political agenda: "Spinning a story involves twisting it to one's advantage, using surrogates, press releases, radio actualities, and other friendly sources to deliver the line from an angle that puts the story in the best possible light. Successful spin often involved getting the media to 'play along' by convincing them—through briefings, backgrounders, or other methods of persuasion—that a particular spin to a story is the correct one."[48]

This brought about the transition from the era of the spin doctors of the 1980s to that of the "story spinners." The neologism was coined by Evan Cornog: "[Democrat adviser] George Stephanopoulos and [Republican adviser] Karl Rove [are] professional story-spinners [who] have helped presidential candidates fashion their stories and identified the best methods of spreading their message."[49] These story spinners now have the subtle task of mobilizing public opinion and turning events into stories. As Cornog explains:

> A presidential campaign is a great festival of narration, with the press serving simultaneously as actor, chorus, and audience. The press interprets stories, has stories reinterpreted for it by political spin doctors, and responds (sometimes) to the public's appetite for new narratives. Campaigns are a high-velocity duel of story versus story that is stretched out over months. New stories must constantly be developed, as old ones are either overturned or lose the public's interest. The successful candidate is the one whose stories connect with the largest number of voters.[50]

While the exercise of presidential power tends to be identified with a sort of uninterrupted election campaign, the criteria for good political communications are increasingly defined by a performative rhetoric (discourses that create facts or situations) whose goal is no longer to transmit information or to explain decisions but to influence the moods and emotions of voters, who are increasingly seen as an audience watching a play. And, in order to do so, it no longer uses arguments or programs, but characters and stories. Democracy becomes something to be stage-managed rather than the exercise of politics.

The ability to structure a political vision by telling stories rather than using rational arguments has become the key to winning and exercising power in media-dominated societies that are awash with rumors, fake news, and disinformation. It is no longer *pertinence* that makes public speech effective but *plausibility*, or the ability to win support, to seduce and to deceive (like the famous "Work more in order to earn more" slogan used by Nicolas Sarkozy during the 2007 French presidential campaign). A candidacy's success no longer depends upon the coherence of an economic program, the pertinence of the solutions that are on offer, or even a lucid vision of what is at stake in geostrategic or ecological terms, but upon the ability to mobilize an audience and retain its loyalty. While the art of the novel consists in a paradoxical enunciation of the truth Aragon defined as "telling true lies," the spin doctors use storytelling as the art of absolute deception, as what we might call "telling false lies," or a new form of disinformation.

Scheherazade's Strategy

American constitutional power has, in the words of the historian Jeffrey K. Tulis, become "a kind of government by assembly without a genuine assembly of the people. In this fictive assembly, television speaks to the president in metaphors expressive of the 'opinion' of the people, and the president responds to the demand and moods created by the media with rhetoric designed to manipulate popular passions rather than to engage citizens in political debate."[51]

It is therefore logical that the election of a new president should look more like the introduction of a fictional character than a political appointment. Once elected, he introduces a certain style, and style has replaced the protocol that once established the order of the ceremonies and introduced the incoming president into a certain institutional order and a hierarchy of precedence and antecedents. The induction of a newly elected president now borrows its metaphors from the order of narrative. Rather than emphasizing the weight of his responsibilities and the burden of power, the talk is of "writing a new page," of a "meeting between a man and a people," or of "the dawn of a new era." A narrative grammar is replacing presidential protocol, and a eulogy of the powers of narrative is replacing the transmission of the "attributes" of power.

As we saw in the introduction, as soon as he entered the White House in January 2001, George W. Bush introduced the members of his government by evoking "stories that really explain what America can and should be about." Five years later in February 2006, after a lightning visit to Afghanistan, he used the same words twice during a press conference: "We like stories, and expect stories, of young girls going to school in Afghanistan." The repetition was not a sign of tiredness. It revealed his adviser Karl Rove's insistence that political life had to be turned into a series of evocative stories and moving tales.

According to Evan Cornog:

> September 11 pushed a new master narrative to the foreground and Bush and his team adroitly seized this new story line and made it theirs, just as in 2000 they had managed to construct a winning campaign around his modest life story. The theme of suffering and redemption was central in both instances. In Bush's personal life, the tale of his struggles with — and victory over — alcohol renders sympathetic a figure who might easily have been perceived as a spoiled rich kid ... the real adversity of the 9/11 attacks permitted Bush to recast ... the new master narrative, which set forth a Manichean struggle between good and evil.[52]

The same technique was exploited *ad nauseam* during the mid-term elections of November 2006, when Bush's ratings were at an all-time low as the US became bogged down in the war in Iraq that had begun three and a half years earlier. According to Ira Chenus, professor of Religious Studies at the University of Colorado, Karl Rove now began to implement "Scheherazade's strategy." The principle behind it is simple: "When policy dooms you, start telling stories — stories so fabulous, so gripping, so spell-binding that the king (or in this case, the American citizen who theoretically rules our country) forgets all about a lethal policy ... The Scheherazade policy ... plays on the insecurity of Americans who feel that their lives are out of control."[53]

During the mid-term elections, Rove was trying to do what he had done so successfully when Bush was re-elected in 2004: distract voters' attention away from the actual record of the war by conjuring up the great collective myths of the American imaginary:

> Karl Rove ... is betting that the voters will be mesmerized by John-Wayne-style tales of "real men" fighting evil on the frontier—at least enough Americans to avoid the death sentences that the voters might otherwise pronounce on the party that brought us to the disaster in Iraq ... So Rove constantly invents simplistic good-against-evil stories for his candidates to tell. He tries to turn every election into a moral drama, a contest of Republican moral clarity against Democratic moral confusion ... The Scheherazade strategy is giant scam, built upon the illusion that simple moralistic tales can make us feel secure, no matter what's actually going on in the world ... Rove wants every vote for a Republican to be a symbolic statement.[54]

Forced by Democratic pressure to resign in August 2007, Karl Rove referred to a novel to describe his situation: "I am Moby Dick, and they are hunting me."[55] His words signaled the apotheosis of a political career that had been completely dedicated to "storytelling," defined as a "politics of illusion" that found its full application in the war which began in Iraq in 2003.

6 Telling War Stories

Twisted rebar, concrete, and splintered furniture lay scattered across the floor of this room. Our view through a jagged hole in the wall looks out on to the city, showing steady civilian traffic crossing a bridge over a river below. Sparrows flap through the grey haze, and Arabic music and the voices of merchants filter up from the street. An army major beside me, Paul Tyrrell, scans the high-rises on the other side of the river through his laser rangefinder. He is the frontline eyes of the coalition, responsible for calling in air strikes. A platoon sergeant named Donald Prado tells Tyrrell that an office tower half a mile to the west is an enemy stronghold.

Virtual Warfare in Baghdad

In eight minutes, coalition soldiers will storm across the bridge. Prado radios in for the air force to drop a smoke screen for cover. He's also spotted snipers on the roof but cautions the major that the civilian facility is off-limits for targeting. Then Tyrrell sees something Prado missed. Three of the antennas on the roof are tactical radio masts, a tip-off that insurgents are using the hospital as a communications base. "That's a high-payoff target, brother," says Tyrrell. He gets approval to deliver a "limited lethality" fragmentation bomb on to the hospital roof. The office tower will receive the full treatment—a 1,000 pound GPS-guided bunker buster. Seconds later, the missiles smash into their targets in perfect synchrony. Smoke and dust billow out in bright plumes, followed by shouts and the keening of ambulance sirens.

The air is thick with heat, but it's not the merciless 120-degree swelter of Baghdad. It's late spring in Lawton, Oklahoma. We're in the battle lab of an Army base called Fort Sill, and the air-conditioning is on the fritz. The river, the bridge, the civilian traffic, the birds, the bombs, and Sergeant Prado are all virtual, a simulation generated by flat-panel displays on the walls, a subwoofer in the floor, and half a dozen Windows and Linux boxes down the hall. Only the smashed furniture, the officer standing beside me, and the adrenaline spikes are real.

So begins Steve Silberman's account. *Wired* magazine's columnist was the first civilian to experience a new form of military training in 2004.[1] The Joint Fires and Effects Training System (JFETS) is a video game based on the immersion of soldiers in semi-virtual worlds that reproduce real combat conditions on the ground in Iraq or Afghanistan. JFETS is the latest in a series of war games and the prototype for "synthetic theaters of war" which combine immersion in an interactive virtual world with a narrative of a story that is lived by characters. There are several different exercises based upon different scenarios, providing high-resolution images, a 360-degree field of vision, and very high quality sound. After spending an hour in this virtual theater, Silberman felt disoriented. "I notice an unexpected after effect of spending an hour in the holodeck. Glancing out a window, my brain no longer trusts that I am seeing the real world. The freeway traffic and trace houses of Marina del Rey seem virtual."

This masterpiece of simulation is the product of unprecedented collaboration between the Pentagon, the University of Southern California, and Hollywood studios under the aegis of the Institute for Creative Technologies (ICT), a think-tank set up in 1999 by the army's Simulation, Training, and Instrumentation Command (STRICOM), with a budget of $45 million. In 2004, ICT's contract with the Pentagon was renewed for a second five-year period, and its budget more than doubled. Housed in futuristic offices designed by a set-designer who once worked on *Star Wars*, ICT's headquarters have always been in a tower near the port of Santa Monica in Los Angeles. It is home to a team of designers, scriptwriters, graphic artists, video designers, researchers working on artificial intelligence, and directors ... all from Hollywood. They are developing simulation models that allow players to behave "as though their experiences were real." Mastery of this type of virtual, interactive, and multisensory environment is now seen as indispensable to the visualization of the battlefield and the training of troops. The founders of the new institute designed it to use the simulation technologies developed by the video-games industry and Hollywood's expert storytellers to devise a new military training system adapted to the strategic issues of the twenty-first century.

When ICT opened, explain Tim Lenoir and Henry Lowood, Army Secretary Louis Caldera said:

> "We could never hope to get the expertise of Steven Spielberg or some of the other film industry people working just on Army projects." But the new institute, Caldera said, will be a "win-win for everyone." ... Flight and tank simulators are excellent tools for learning and practicing the use of complex, expensive equipment. However, movies, theme park rides and increasingly even video games are driven by stories with plot, feeling, tension, and emotion. To train for real world military engagements is not just to train on how to use the equipment but how to cope with the implementation of strategy in an environment with uncertainties, surprises, and participants with actual fears.[2]

This was not the first time the Pentagon had used simulation techniques and special effects to train its soldiers. Hollywood had already produced military training films, and the universities are accustomed to signing contracts with the US Army. To take only one famous example: in 1965, the Department of Defense commissioned a computer simulation game called "Politica" for Project Camelot. Designed by the Cambridge-based research organization Abt Associates, "The game was first loaded with data about hundreds of social psychological variables in a given country: degree of group cohesiveness, levels of self-esteem, attitudes toward authority, and so on. Then it would highlight those variables decisive for the description, indication, and control of internal revolutionary conflict."[3]

The simulation was in fact about Chile, where Salvador Allende had come close to winning the previous year's election. A few years later, it was to outline the CIA's role in the process that led to the bloody overthrow on the Popular Unity government on September 11, 1973.

In the 1990s, the very existence of STRICOM was testimony to the Pentagon's determination not to be left behind in terms of simulation and special-effects technology, and to exploit the new technologies and products of the entertainment industries (movies, video games, theme parks, etc.). But this joint venture between Hollywood and the Pentagon was based on an unprecedented agreement; for the first time a multi-disciplinary production structure was developed on the Department of Defense's initiative. As *The Village Voice*'s film critic Ed Halter remarked in 2002, it was as though the military had tried to develop its own studio in the 1930s, and as though that studio had become one of the big players in the cinematographic industry.[4]

From Cold War to Fake War

The establishment of the ICT was the culmination of a long process of collaboration between the Pentagon and the Hollywood studios, but it was primarily a response to the new strategic issues that had emerged since the end of the Cold War. In the early 1990s, the US Army had to face new challenges: in an age of urban warfare and the struggle against terrorism, decisions had to be taken lower and lower down the chain of command. Teaching new recruits to shoot and to march in step was therefore no longer enough.

Interviewed in February 2000, STRICOM's scientific director Michael M. Macedonia—who was one of the main architects behind this strategic turn—told the *New York Times*:

> The model was: "Go prepare for the cold war on the central front in Europe—mass Soviet armies." That model doesn't exist any more. Essentially, the missions that we do in the Army are very complex today. Look at Kosovo, look at Bosnia, look at what we had to do in Haiti. The fact is that our soldiers have to learn to work in a disciplined process and have some empathy and have some understanding of the cultures and of the people and of the context that they're in.[5]

The end of the Cold War completely changed the nature of the army's missions. New fields of intervention have emerged in American strategic doctrine. "Operations other than war," for example, include interceding between rival factions after a ceasefire, distributing humanitarian goods and services, deploying multinational forces, supervising elections, supplying humanitarian aid during a conflict or after a natural disaster, building states by training police and security forces, helping to build infrastructures, supervising disarmament, creating humanitarian corridors, destroying coca or opium fields, supporting "fragile democratic states," the struggle against rogue states, the war on terror, urban guerrilla warfare, and much more.

"It became apparent during the first Gulf War," Nick Gillette wrote in the *Guardian*, "that American soldiers were being needlessly exposed to the risk of death and serious injury through lack of training in urban combat. Realizing that this mode of fighting was likely to become even more prevalent, the US Army decided to educate recruits in military operations in urban terrain (or MOUT)."[6]

There were budgetary constraints as well as new strategic conditions: after the collapse of the Soviet Union, public opinion and Congress began to demand the "peace dividend," or major cuts in a defense budget that seemed to be quite irrelevant to the new geostrategic context. It fell by 13 percent during the 1990s. On the basis of military information predicting the closure of military bases and the cancellation of long-term projects a Congressional office of assessment estimated in 1992 that 2.5 million defense-related jobs would be eliminated between 1991 and 2002.[7]

These budgetary restrictions forced the army to change its training systems. Large-scale maneuvers with hundreds of thousands of men in real situations, like the "Reforger" programme of 1988 that mobilized 175,000 men in Germany at a cost of $53.9 billion, were now out of the question. The new "Reforger" programme of 1992, which was based upon the new cooperative capabilities acquired thanks to the simulation programmes adopted by the army and especially the air force, mobilized only 6,500 soldiers (who simulated 175,000 men) at a cost of $19.5 million.[8]

Growing reliance on reservists is a further argument in favor of simulated exercises: they made it possible to organize "at home" training weekends. Reservists can use the new systems from their home bases and prepare for complex operations before they are mobilized. This considerably improves the quality of their training.

"Whereas during the cold war American forces had been dispersed to fixed forward bases abroad, future missions will require rapid deployment of small flexible forces to trouble spots around the world. Finally, the army may have to fight in joint operations with multinational forces, with or without United Nations or foreign senior command over its soldiers."[9]

It is striking to note that, during the 1990s, America's military organization experienced the same restructuring process as the big bureaucratic and hierarchical firms (see chapters 2 and 3 above). The collapse of the old Fordist model, which was bound up with the industrial capitalism of the postwar period, and the emergence of a new model that was decentralized, flexible, and structured into networks, affected the army too. It too conformed to the paradigm of an organization made up of supposedly autonomous individuals who could take decisions and adapt to an uncertain environment. And it had to be able to adapt to the changing situation as the conjuncture changed by constantly inventing new forms of cooperation that were limited in terms of both time and space.

" 'We have been able to demonstrate for several years now the use of networked simulations,' said Michael Macedonia. 'There has always been a goal, for example, to link up 100,000 players. But we've never really done that.' "[10]

The fact remains that, as early as 1995, the Pentagon had decided to codify its new rules and training techniques by developing a new system known as Distributed Mission Training. DMT created virtual theaters of war by connecting the players to real-time simulators that generated synthetic environments by using the latest advances in virtual reality technology.[11]

The air force was obviously the first to implement this reform in the 1990s, when it replaced individual flight-simulation systems with networked simulations that allowed several people to take part and to share tasks. Robert Haffa Jr. and James H. Patton Jr. summed up the changes in an article published in the *Army War College Quarterly* in 1998: "Traditional military missions, once separated in time, distance, platform, and function, are now being fused. This integration of surveillance, information, battle management, and precision strike has become known over the last few years as a 'system of systems.' "[12]

In his 2000 interview with the *New York Times*, Michael Macedonia stated:

You look at what Sony is doing, or Microsoft or Electronic Arts, and although their technology is imperfect, they are rapidly refining it. Basically, they are providing those large-scale virtual environments. And we can call them games. But they really are large-scale collaborative virtual environments where people can express themselves. They are defining how the technology will go, and they are also defining the art. That is, how do you create the content for these virtual environments, and the expectations of what people will see in them. We find that very intriguing. The problem, oddly, is that most computer games are too militaristic for the Army. In Command and Conquer, for instance, you amass huge stockpiles of weapons and train legions of soldiers for an all-out, full-face assault. But that sort of confrontation is no longer in the Pentagon playbook.[13]

All the more reason for the Pentagon to develop its own games…

The Issue of "Realism"

In 1997, two years before the ICT was set up, a conference in Monterey, California, brought together video-games specialists and military trainers. They were to lay the foundations for an institutional collaboration designed to share advances in graphic design, sound effects, human–machine interfaces, and virtual immersion. And yet the military and the representatives from the entertainment industries had their differences from the very beginning.

Oddly enough, their differences were not about ethical or political issues (Hollywood's involvement in a war went almost unchallenged), and still less were they about strategic issues (their conception of modern warfare). They had to do with aesthetic questions and, more specifically, their respective views as to the meaning of *realism* when it came to simulation, imitation, or virtual immersion. Whereas the military had a photographic conception of realism, the video-games specialists put the emphasis on the credibility of the stories that were being told. That controversy has been part of the aesthetic debate ever since the days of Plato and Aristotle, but it was also an expression of an old struggle between the army and Hollywood over who should have the monopoly of representation.

In his book *War and Cinema*, Paul Virilio recalls that Joseph Goebbels wanted to outrival Hollywood.[14] His civil defense advisers used columns of light to simulate cities, thus illustrating the old collusion/rivalry between war and cinema, which both involve stage management. The new simulation tools used by the US Army to train its troops confirmed what Paul Virilio was saying when his book was first published in French in 1984: the battlefield is not just a space of combat but also a representational space. From Ordnance Survey maps to the first aerial photographs taken during the First World War to today's satellite images, weapons of war have always been used alongside instruments for optical or cartographic *reconnaissance* that can reconnoiter the theaters of operations, locate the enemy, record losses, and ascertain what damage has been inflicted on the enemy. Virilio writes:

> The functions of the weapon and the eye merge in the sights of guns and the ranger-finders of long-range artillery. Nadar's invention of the first systematic aerostatic photography in 1858, and aerial photo-interpretation during the First World War, are perfect illustrations of the cinematic dimension of the destruction that is inflicted on whole regions, of the never-ending destruction of a landscape that must be immediately reconstructed with the help of series of photographs, and the cinematic pursuit of uncertain territories in which film replaces the staff's maps.[15]

The technical refinement of optical instruments is a response to the "tactical" demand for visibility and encourages attempts to make the battlefield transparent by developing night-vision systems, satellite images, GPS navigation, target-guided missiles. At the same time, there is a growing need to deceive the enemy by using decoys. The increased use of optical technology—lighting up targets, night-time air raids, flares—and the growing use of visual decoys transform battlefields into real film sets, battles into a series of special effects, and troop movements into choreography.

"Soldiers' perceptions have for decades been technically mediated by computers and other aids embedded in various weapons systems," notes Sharon Ghamari-Tabrizi, "but the augmented reality systems of DMT go beyond making the synthetic environment appear as close as possible to the actual sphere of combat and change soldiers' perceptions of the actual battlespace."[16]

Seeing is not enough to do that; we have to *believe in* a virtual world. When we are fighting a war, we cannot trust what we see: the goal is not just to win territory, but also to win minds.

The never-ending refinement of visual and representational systems has, however, a paradoxical effect. As Jean Baudrillard remarked of the first Gulf War, it encourages incredulity. Seeing was once proof that things were real. The credibility of images fades as they become more widely available. Seeing is no longer enough; we have to believe a story.

One participant in the 1997 conference in Monterey recalled: "Whereas the DOD [Department of Defense] has tended to emphasize the fidelity of interactions between objects in a simulated environment (using science-based models), the entertainment industry has tended to promote visual fidelity and uses principles of *good storytelling* to help participants suspend their disbelief about the reality of a synthetic experience."[17] Another remarked: "In this view, the goal of a simulation is not to approximate reality as nearly as possible, but to present individuals with the appropriate set of clues to produce the training effect desired."[18]

For his part, the Walt Disney Company's Danny Hills explained: "If you want to make someone frightened, it is not sufficient to show them a frightening picture. You have to spend a lot of time setting them up with the right music, with cues, with camera angles, things like that, so that when you put that frightening picture up, they are startled."[19]

The team led by Paramount Digital Entertainment's Richard Lindheim (who was to become the ICT's first director) emphasized that the role played by the story and characters in a science-fiction video made in 1997 was much more decisive than the technology: "Video and audio are the means to help you get to know the characters. But it is the characters and the stories that draw the participant into the event and create a compelling feeling that it *is* 2010 and these are *real* crises."[20]

"Do We Have the Right Story?"

In his 2004 article, *Wired*'s Steve Silberman explained: "The architect of the current wave of innovation is Michael Macedonia, the head of the Army's simulation office":

Macedonia takes a long view of his work. "People have been using simulation for thousands of years, as long as there's been a military.

They told stories, drew pictures in the sand, invented chess," he says. "They made these abstractions in the hopes that they could understand the nature and dynamics of war ... Now all these modes are converging in the new breed of training simulations," he says. Macedonia draws a parallel between the real-life combat scenarios employed by ICT and the epics of Homer—tales told to pass on the wisdom of seasoned warriors to those who are called to fight ... "The big challenge isn't getting the technology right," Macedonia tells me. "We're almost there. The challenge is, Do we have the right story? Does it map to reality? Are we teaching the right thing? The real story of warfare is that your buddy's dying—what do you do?[21]

In October 1996, a workshop financed by the National Research Council (NRC) brought together representatives of the leisure, movie, and video-games industries, members of the Department of Defense, and academics.[22] All those involved in the new media thought that the best way to achieve experimental immersion in the electronic media was not hypertext, but the good old techniques of storytelling. Alex Seiden of the special-effects and animation company Industrial Light and Magic explained: "I've never seen a CD-ROM that moved me the way a powerful film has. I've never visited a Web page with great emotional impact. I contend that linear narrative is the fundamental art form of humankind: the novel, the play, the film ... these are the forms that define our cultural experience."[23]

They do in fact now make it possible to get players to enter a virtual environment by fostering the illusion that it is a real world. The credibility of simulation exercises is based upon "the perception that a world exists into which participants can port themselves and undertake some actions." The NRC report on the workshop describes the "human operator's relationship to the synthetic environment as 'experiential rather than cognitive.'"[24] Storytelling appears, then, to be the key to making these virtual worlds "credible." Unless they are credible, the simulation is still a game that is played at a distance and not an effective form of training that can trigger the desired attitudes and aptitudes in the subjects who are being trained.

As the French political scientist Maurice Ronai explains, Paramount Digital Entertainment began to collaborate with the air force's Defense Modeling and Simulation Office (DMSO). Their goal was to "train officers to take decisions in times of crisis." The new techniques had to put troops "in situation" and prepare them to make decisions in remote combat zones. To that end, "Paramount Digital and the University of California's Information Sciences Institute developed a 'situation generator' known as the Story Drive Engine." [25]

The "Story Drive" Project

In 1999, ICT decided to develop two prototype simulations: a mission designed to rehearse maneuvers, and one for leadership training. "ICT's deputy technology director explains that to teach recruits how to navigate complex situations, ICT's training packages are built around the oldest form of immersive experience: storytelling." [26] Both prototypes therefore include storylines for each simulation — complete with character profiles, simulated environmental conditions (wind, temperature, humidity, and smells) — a game for the networked training, to be played in virtual theaters of war inside the ICT building.

This tool was tested at the Industrial college of the Armed Forces in an exercise code-named "Final Flurry." A group of officers were presented with multi-media story lines: the officers were plunged into a crisis in the Middle East as Iran and the United States came into conflict against a background of nuclear war between India and Pakistan. The officers' reactions were immediately converted into realistic images and text. When an officer launched a naval attack in the Straits of Hormuz, the system immediately generated real-time images from ZNN-TV, an imaginary replica of CNN. At the end of the exercise, the officers drew conclusions from the exercise and explained them to an equally imaginary President of the Republic. [27]

Every morning, they were given the day's storyline, which included a set of geopolitical data, and private and public commentaries. On this basis, the players had to define the appropriate national security policy. The interactive nature of the exercise made it a learning experience that exposed erroneous data, missed opportunities, illusions, deceptions, etc.

The game's novel feature was that it left the players free to determine their course of action, while allowing the director to orchestrate how they behaved. Discussing the problems inherent in this kind of virtual reality theater, Margaret Thomas Kelso and her collaborators explain: "We wanted to know if the interactor could be guided without feeling manipulated. We believe that providing a satisfactory experience for an interactor relies on maintaining a delicate balance between freedom and control ... allowing the interactor maximum freedom of choice while still presenting a shaped experience."[28] Michael Macedonia, who was one of the project's founders, explains: "By exercising control of these elements, the Director ensures that the exercise follows the intended story line so that the intended training goals can be achieved."[29]

For his part, Larry Tuch, Paramount's manager for the demonstration project, stressed the importance of interactivity:

> In the *Story Drive* experience the students are more like a movie audience with the teachers as the director. He can orchestrate story events by sending the students e-mail, voice mail or electronic video mail, and specific information in the form of television newsclips, briefing documents, maps, and intelligence reports. But, of course, this is more than a movie. And that means the students also have the power to react to and affect the direction of the story.

We are a long way from the video games in which the player is a shooter who has to kill as many victims as possible. Computer-programmed storylines mobilize all the players' senses—sight, hearing, touch, and smell—and allow them to come face to face with real characters that can, in theory, react to the situation exactly as real human beings would react. Rather than having to put up with the bellowing of a Sergeant Hartman, from Stanley Kubrick's film *Full Metal Jacket*, the soldiers can talk to an intelligent robot within the video game. The danger of this kind of immersion has to do with the fact that the player is stimulated so as to achieve a high level of concentration. Some psychologists think that these techniques can have terrible effects: there is a great danger that they will produce soldiers who are over-trained, dehumanized, and who have no sense of compassion or pity. They may create cyborg warriors who are cut off from the real world and trained to kill—as we have seen in Iraq since 2003.

In June 2006, *Time* magazine revealed that US Marines had perpetrated a massacre in Haditha on November 19, 2005. Some 100 kilometers north of Baghdad, twenty-four civilians—including ten women and children who were executed at point-blank range—were killed in cold blood by the Marines. The main accused, twenty-six-year-old Sergeant Frank Wuterich, was accused of murdering twelve people and ordering the massacre of another six.[30] At his trial in December 2006, Wuterich's lawyer told the court that the Marines had simply done what they had been trained to do.

"By turning to Hollywood in the 1990s, the military has not shifted its authority for shaping the subjectivity of its forces from seasoned professionals to the Scheherazades of sensation and sentiment," Sharon Ghamri-Tabrizi concludes in her study of the convergence of the Pentagon and Hollywood. "But," she adds, not without a certain naiveté, "it is important to remember that when the simulation tests more senior command levels and strategic policy making, what is needed most is depth and complexity in the crisis scenario. Leaders must be trained to deliberate over the relevant information, not to respond with a spasm of primal emotion."[31]

"Weapons of Mass Distraction"

According to Richard Lindheim, Paramount Digital Entertainment's vice-president and the man behind ICT, the Vietnam generation had been raised on television, whereas the young soldiers of today have grown up on video games. An army study shows that 90 percent of the 75,000 young men who enlist every year have already used video games, and 30 percent regard themselves as "hardcore gamers."[32] Faced with a serious shortage of volunteers, the US Army relies upon a vast audience of hardcore gamers to make up for the shortfall. Launched on the army's website on July 4, 2002, *America's Army* (www.americasarmy.com) is used by its recruitment sections. Available free on the Internet, it is one of the five most popular online video games. A presentation by its designer Mike Zyda leaves no doubt as to its intentions: "Weapons of Mass Distraction—America's Army recruits for real war."[33]

The game includes links to the www.goarmy.com site that allows players to explore the possibility of a career in the military and to contact a recruiter. According to Colonel Casey Wardynski, the game was downloaded by 6.1 million users in 2005. Its effectiveness as a recruitment tool is undeniable: between 20 and 40 percent of new recruits to the army had already played the game. "Instead of moving the classroom into the field, we're moving the field into the classroom," said ICT's deputy technology director Randy Hill.[34]

As Heather Chaplin and Aaron Ruby explain in their book *Smartbomb* (2005),[35] *America's Army* is not just an excellent PR and recruitment tool; it is also a way of testing a recruit's military aptitudes. Mike Zyda admits that its designers did seriously think of using players' aptitudes and profiles to recruit them directly. That suggestion was not taken up, but players who request information about a career in the military reveal their usernames to the recruiters and may find that their performances have been correlated with their real identities with a view to enlisting them into the army.

In an article published in the British *Guardian* in 2005, the games designer Greg Costikian baldly stated: "Given that we have a volunteer military, the military needs to recruit. And if it's legitimate for them to use TV and print advertising, what's wrong with doing so through a game?"[36]

Another article in the same newspaper made the cautious suggestion that: "If you were a sensationalist, you might describe this colonization of youth entertainment as the biggest militarization of an adolescent population since the Hitler Youth."[37]

Video games are therefore not just used to train soldiers. They are used in recruitment drives, and they are also a valuable way of treating Post-Traumatic Stress Disorder in troops who have come back from the front. One of ICT's projects is designed to help veterans overcome the problems that, according to a study by the Walter Reed Army Institute of Research dating from 2004, affect more than 15 percent of combat personnel returning from Iraq.[38] The ICT's website informs us that this program consists in using the "environment as the basis of treatment, whereby a veteran with PTSD can experience a combat-relevant scenario in a low-threat context to therapeutically process emotion and decondition the effects of the disorder." The *Guardian*'s James Verini describes the process: "By recycling virtual graphic assets built for the combat tactical simulation game, Full Spectrum Warrior and other ICT assets, the project is able to build prototypes quickly and cost-effectively … to help veterans overcome the effects of PTSD and restore quality of life to them and their families."[39]

According to Robert McLay, a Navy psychiatrist specializing in the therapeutic application of virtual reality, therapy for trauma often requires visits to the actual scene of the assault: " "You don't want to send someone who is traumatized back to Iraq. This allows us to bring someone back, but within the situation here." And, he said, some PTSD sufferers are unable or unwilling to recall things in counseling sessions without stimuli, such as the digital images of a combat hospital, a recorded Islamic prayer melody or the smell of cordite explosives misted into a psychologist's office.[40]

On February 9, 2007, the *LA Times* journalist Larry Gordon revealed that the National Institute of Mental Health was funding a $2 million study at Emory School of Medicine using a virtual Iraq in combination with the drug D-cycloserine, which has been shown to reduce the fear of heights.[41] Both combat training and trauma therapy obey the same rules: immersion in a virtual world. For ICT, treating traumatized soldiers and training men to fight is the same thing.

War: A Counter-Narrative

It may seem even more astonishing, but it is very logical in this context: the way storytelling and the virtualization of reality through digital technologies have transformed representations of war has had a profound influence on American politicians' "worldviews" and the way they make decisions faced with the complexity of global geopolitics and the challenges posed by "hyper-terrorism."

A few days after the 9/11 attacks, the international press reported that a meeting had taken place between senior officials from the Department of Defense and a number of Hollywood screenwriters and directors. They included John Milius (who co-wrote *Apocalypse Now*), Steven E. De Souza (the co-writer of *Die Hard*), and, more surprisingly, Randal Kleiser (who directed the musical *Grease*). The group's findings have never been made public, but the press repeated the official line that the purpose of the meeting had been to ask Hollywood's screenwriters to come up with possible scenarios for a future terrorist attack and possible responses to it.

The idea that screenwriters and directors can predict the future and act as advisers to the government in the same way that the Delphic oracle or Roman chiromancers did is so typical of Hollywood that it has inspired many films and novels. In Sidney Pollack's *Three Days of the Condor* (1975), adapted from James Grady's bestselling novel, the main character Joseph Turner (Robert Redford) works for a New York CIA branch operating under the cover of a so-called "Society for American Literary History." His task, along with that of his colleagues, is to read every novel published in every language in search of possible scenarios or leaks. Their notes are then recorded on a computer and centralized further up the hierarchy. All the leads are compared with the CIA's data and intelligence to detect possible overlaps with signs of subversive activity.

In the days that followed 9/11, there was much discussion of the predictions made in Tom Clancy's novels and the storylines of disaster movies such as *The Towering Inferno* or, more recently, the *Die Hard* trilogy, in which Bruce Willis confronts terrorists in various situations. The fact that three biggest hits of the 1990s — *Independence Day* (Roland Emmerich, 1996), *Armageddon* (Michael Bay, 1998), and *Deep Impact* (Mimi Leader, 1998) — all deal with mass destruction was grist for the mill for those who believe in predictions and premonitions, as are news stories such as the murder of John Lennon in December 1980. On the day of the murder, his killer Mark David Chapman was carrying J. D. Salinger's novel *Catcher in the Rye* as though it was a prayer book. Then there is John Hinckley, who tried to assassinate President Ronald Reagan in 1981, and who claimed to be another of the novel's fans.

The one thing that all these episodes have in common is the idea that fiction anticipates reality. The same idea reappears in Steven Spielberg's film *Minority Report* (2002), adapted from a remarkable short story by Philip K. Dick. Brains that have been plunged into an artificial vegetative state have dreams that allow them to foresee, or actually *see*, images of crimes before they are committed. The criminals can then be arrested before they have done anything. In Paul Verhoeven's *Starship Troopers* (1997), where the world is under a complete American hegemony after "an immense reshaping of the world," the agents of "psyCorps" — a sort of high tech Gestapo — are capable of telling the future. They can read their enemies' minds and influence the people they tune into. This, writes Jean-Michel Valentin, is "a metaphor for the infodominance capacity that Space Command is trying to develop."[42]

Paradoxically, the task of deconstructing this illusion fell to the novelist Don DeLillo. Having described a fictional firm (see Chapter 3 above), he now describes American society as a world that is saturated in fictions, under a spell, and "Quixotic" in the sense that it prefers fiction to reality and that its most famous "heroes" (Kennedy, Hoover, Nixon, Sinatra, Monroe, Oswald...) behave as though they were fictional characters. This is how DeLillo's novel *Libra* describes the fictional character he calls "Win Everett," a former CIA agent and the brains behind the plot against John F. Kennedy:

> Win Everett was at work devising a general shape, a life. He would create a gunman out of ordinary dog-eared paper ... An address book with ambiguous leads. Photographs expertly altered (or crudely altered). Letters, travel documents, counterfeit signatures, a history of false names. It would all require a massive decipherment, a conversion to plain text. He envisaged teams of linguists, photo analysts, fingerprint experts, handwriting experts, experts in hairs and fibers, smudges and blurs. Investigators building up chronologies. He would give them the makings of deep chronos, lead them to basement rooms in windy industrial slums, to lost towns in the Tropics ... Win would scratch onto these miniature pages enough trails, false trails, swarming life, lingering mysteries, enough real and fabricated people to occupy investigators for months to come ... You have to leave them with coincidence, lingering mystery. This is what makes it real ... They wanted a name, a face, a bodily frame they might use to extend their fiction into the world.[43]

The meeting between officials from the Department of Defense and Hollywood screenwriters was quite in keeping with the unreal atmosphere of a post-9/11 period in which fictions and indoctrination flourish. It was not held in the Pentagon, but at the Institute of Creative Technologies in Los Angeles. The man who organized the meeting was none other than Karl Rove, the architect of "Scheherazade's strategy" who was to preside over the post-9/11 reconfiguration of the world, spread his fictions throughout the world, and busy himself with the unresolved mysteries and coincidences that make things real. Rove was the man behind the new transfictional policy of "war storytelling." Anything that the terrorists had destroyed could be rebuilt by the architects of Scheherazade's strategy: a counter-narrative.

Hollywood and the Pentagon Work Together

There were more and more indications of collusion between Hollywood and the Pentagon, especially after September 11, 2001. At the beginning of January 2002, Vice-President Dick Cheney and Defense Secretary Donald Rumsfeld attended the Washington premiere of Scott Ridley's film *Black Hawk Down*, which "fictionalizes" the US Army's fiasco in Somalia in 1993 (overseas American bases were sent cassettes of the film). When *We Were Soldiers* was released in March 2002, a private screening was organized for George W. Bush, Donald Rumsfeld, and Condoleezza Rice; it is a very patriotic account of the battle between American and North Vietnamese forces at Drang in 1965. And in 2003, the Pentagon used Phil Alden Robinson's *The Sum of All Fears* (2002) in its recruitment drive. Robinson had been given access to Pentagon and CIA files that were classified "confidential."

But that is not all, as Samuel Blumenfeld described in an article in *Le Monde* in 2002: "Attorney General John Ashcroft waited until the Monday following the second weekend of the release of *The Sum of All Fears* to announce the arrest of the terrorist Abdullah al-Mujahir, or José Padilla to use his original name. He had links with al-Qaeda and had been plotting an attack similar to that described in Phil Alden Robinson's film. Stranger still, John Ashcroft happened to be in Moscow when the arrest was announced, as though to echo the ending of *The Sum of All Fears*, in which Russian–American cooperation saves the world from chaos."[44]

War storytelling cannot, however, be reduced to purely ideological affects or to a set of deceptions designed to conceal economic or military interests. Such ideological affects do not fall from the skies; they are grounded in institutions, practices, and powers. ICT is an important actor in war storytelling, but it is also a laboratory for testing new forms of cooperation between knowledge-disciplines and power-technologies. It is experimenting with new paradigms for leadership, training, education, and mobilization, and with new ways of articulating the handling of weapons and the training of individuals, and relations between simulation technologies and the cognitive sciences.

When the Hollywood studios began to describe themselves as an "industry," it was an indication that films were undergoing a process of industrialization. Storytelling is now the object of an equivalent process:

in the Hollywood-like setting of the ICT and thanks to the magic of virtual realities, new technologies of power are being developed. They allow the military institution to not only "discipline and punish, as it did in the disciplinary society described by Michel Foucault, but to use fictional war to train and control, to recruit and mobilize.

This overall structure articulates discursive forms and practices (training, recruitment, storylines, and software) with investments and markets. It is what Tim Lenoir and Henry Lockwood described, in an article that has often been cited here, a military-entertainment complex. The expression alludes to the "military-industrial complex" described by President Eisenhower (1953–61) after the Second World War. Eisenhower's complex has not vanished, as we might have thought for a moment at the end of the Cold War, and has in part been restructured around the new technologies and the virtual industries. "Indeed," they write, "a cynic might argue that whereas the military-industrial complex was more or less visible and identifiable during the Cold War, today it is invisibly present, permeating our daily lives."[45]

According to Lenoir and Lockwood, the ICT and other agencies (Waves, Mitre Cooperation) are the visible part of this new complex. They focus on activities that are wrongly described as entertainment (their goal is not to entertain, but to mobilize). Thanks to the explosion of new transmission and visualization technologies, they became strategic; they are now subsumed under the category of digital storytelling. This is a new complex of activities, and it has its own production offices, special-effects studios, budgets calculated in billions of dollars, and cutting-edge technologies (weapons, artificial intelligence, cognitive sciences).

The old theater of war, with its rules and spatio-temporal constraints, its logistics, the "visual" genius of its strategists and the physical courage of its soldiers, has given way to virtual battlefields and "augmented reality" systems. These create a new hybrid environment in which wars are no longer fought on a real battlefield but amongst a proliferation of signs. This virtual warfare is fought not with weapons, but with data, systems for decoding information, and storylines whose ultimate goal is not so much the annihilation of the enemy as the mythical construction of the enemy.

"Cooperation between Hollywood and the Pentagon has allowed the new genre of the national security thriller to emerge," writes Maurice Ronai, and its narratives involve "asymmetrical challenges" such as hijacked missiles, stolen nuclear warheads, the proliferation of biological weapons or cyber blackmail. But while the screenwriters are very inventive when it comes to describing the "threats" and "crises," their descriptions of the enemy are very sloppy: it is always the mafia, a terrorist group, a rogue state. The "crisis" is handled at the highest level of the American government (increasingly personified by the national security adviser, when it is not the president himself), but it is played out on the ground, with the intervention of special forces.[46]

Redeploying the battlefield by modifying perceptions is no longer enough; we have to create what reception theorists call a "horizon of expectation" for the war. The war effort has to a large extent become a story that justifies torture and the deployment of special forces on the ground, explains and demonstrates new weapons, and tests and promotes transmission and visualization technologies—films, video games, TV series, and the media are the fictional vectors for this mobilization drive. Storytelling is its operational mode and, as the title of the cult series about the hero Jack Bauer openly boasts, it works in real time, 24 hours a day.

24: Fiction Normalizes States of Emergency

The worldwide success of this American series cannot be explained solely in terms of the nature of the events it describes—the desperate attempts of the Los Angeles-based Counter Terrorist Unit to thwart an attack that could have unpredictable consequences—or even in terms of the parallel montage of the various story lines, which heightens the tension. The explanation lies in the way it uses real time to enmesh the viewer in both narrative and temporal terms. Each season consists of 24 hour-long episodes covering the events of a single day. The length of the commercial breaks is part of the episode's temporality, which is materialized by the on-screen presence of a digital clock. The temporality of the action is therefore perfectly synchronized with that of its perception. The synchronization of fiction and reality does away with the temporal and symbolic distance that is characteristic of all representation. Events are shown both as they are lived and as they are represented, acted out, and perceived without any distance, and in a synchronization that makes it possible to fuse virtuality and reality.

The action is no longer conjugated in the imperfect tense of fiction, but in a new tense designed to convey a sense of normalized urgency or a permanent state of emergency which, as the Slovene philosopher Slavoj Žižek remarks, involves more than a suspension of moral judgment ("a kind of suspension of ordinary moral concerns"). According to Žižek, this state of emergency takes the form of an injunction to use torture as something "that simply has to be done" in circumstances of normalized emergency. There is no need to be hung up about it: the new law allows everyone to interrogate everyone else—fathers can torture sons, husbands can torture wives, and sisters can torture brothers—in order to obtain information that concerns everyone. This, observes Žižek in an allusion to Kundera's "realm where moral judgment is suspended" (he is referring to the novel), is a "sad indication of a deep change in our ethical and political standards."[47]

The real issue is the prescriptive nature of Hollywood's fictions and their function, which is to justify actions that are unconstitutional or simply immoral. The invention of a social model in which federal agents —real or fictional—must have enough autonomy to act in order to protect the population adequately is nothing other than the establishment of a permanent state of exception which, because it cannot be justified in legal or constitutional terms, seeks and finds its legitimacy in fiction.

Should further proof be required, it has already been provided by Antonin Scalia—a judge sitting in the US Supreme Court and with a duty to respect the Constitution—at a legal conference held in Ottawa in June 2007. He justified the use of torture, not on the basis of an analysis of legal texts, but by using the example of Jack Bauer. Thinking of the second season, in which we see the hero save California from a nuclear attack thanks to information obtained during interrogations involving torture, he boldly asserted: "Jack Bauer saved Los Angeles ... He saved hundreds of thousands of lives. Are you going to convict Jack Bauer? ... Say that criminal law is against him? You have the right to a jury trial? Is any jury going to convict Jack Bauer? I don't think so. So the question is really whether you believe in those absolutes. And ought we believe in these absolutes."[48]

The fact that an eminent judge sitting in the Supreme Court—the institution which, in theory, guarantees that the laws and actions of the executive are constitutional—can claim to use a TV series as an argument to justify the validity of acts of torture that are illegal under international law, and thus establishes what has to be called "Jack Bauer jurisprudence," indicates how far political life had degenerated under the Bush administration. As we shall see, the effects of this "Jack Bauer jurisdiction" are being felt at the highest levels of government and the state, where American business's power to fictionalize the real world, allows prejudice to triumph over the most basic morality, and allows the omnipotence of representations that claim to be transforming the real world to negate its existence.

7 The Propaganda Empire

In an article published in the *New York Times Magazine* a few days before the 2004 presidential election, Ron Suskind, the author of several investigations into White House communications after 2000 and a former op-ed columnist on the *Wall Street Journal* described a conversation he had with one of George W. Bush's aides in the summer of 2002.

"We're An Empire … And We Create Our Own Reality"

The aide, who had not liked the article about Bush's former communications director Karen Hughes that Suskind had written for *Esquire*, took him to task in unexpected terms:

> The aide said that guys like me were "in what we call the reality-based community," which he defined as people who "believe that solutions emerge from your judicious study of discernible reality." I nodded and murmured something about enlightenment principles and empiricism. He cut me off. "That's not the way the world really works anymore," he continued. "We're an empire now, and when we act, we create our own reality. And while you're studying that reality—judiciously, as you will—we'll act again, creating other new realities, which you can study too, and that's how things will sort out. We're history's actors … and you, all of you, will be left to just study what we do.[1]

These comments from a high-level American political figure (probably Karl Rove) are not just cynical or worthy of a media Machiavelli; they seem to have come from a stage play and not an office in the White Office. They do not just raise a political or diplomatic problem. They are not just a new version of the old dilemmas that have always haunted the corridors of power or of the debates between pragmatists and idealists, realists and moralists, hawks and doves or, in 2002, between the defenders of international law and those who wanted to resort to force. They reveal a new conception of relations between politics and reality: the leaders of the most powerful nation in the world were turning away not only from *Realpolitik* but from realism itself, and were beginning to create their own reality, to control appearances, and to promote what might be called a fictional *Realpolitik*.

Already invested with the supernatural power to heal (or to tend the wounds of a nation damaged by terrorism, as we saw in Chapter 5) that was once attributed to the kings studied by Marc Bloch,[2] the American executive was being granted a truly "divine" ability by a White House spin doctor: it would constantly create new "realities" that were inaccessible to reason and observation.

Suskind's article caused a sensation. Op-ed writers and bloggers seized on the expression "reality-based community," which spread across the Web—in July 2007, Google picked up over one million references to it. Wikipedia has a page devoted to it. According to Jay Rosen, professor of Journalism at New York University, "Many on the left *adopted* the term. 'Proud member of the reality-based community,' their blogs said. The right then *jeered* at the left's self-description. (*They're* reality-based? Yeah, right.')"[3]

It was a perfect example of what the *New York Times* executive director Bill Keller defined as an "intellectual scoop": "When you can look at all the dots everyone can look at, and be the first to connect them in a meaningful and convincing way, that's something."[4] In his long commentary on Suskind's piece, Jay Rosen went so far as to say: "The only piece of political journalism ever to make me cry was Ron Suskind's article … I felt an immediate kinship with Suskind. Because I could see what he was trying to do: warn us about something that sounded crazy but that was all too real. I could see he was going to fail in that, and I sensed that he knew it too. That's what made it so sad to read."

Rosen explained:

Over the last three years, and ever since the adventure in Iraq began, Americans have seen spectacular failures of intelligence, spectacular collapses in the press, spectacular breakdowns in the reality-checks built into government, including the evaporation of oversight in

Congress, and the by-passing of the National Security Council, which was created to prevent exactly these events ... Reduced deliberation, oversight, fact-finding, and field reporting were different elements of an emerging political style. Suskind, I felt, got to the sense of it with his phrase, "the retreat from empiricism..." A different pattern had appeared under George W. Bush and Dick Cheney. The normal checks and balances had been overcome, so that executive power could flow more freely.[5]

The government's reaction to Suskind's article was proportional to its impact. According to Eric Boehlert, writing in the webzine *Salon*: "Bush aides once welcomed reporter Ron Suskind into the White House ... Today, Suskind may rank near the top of the administration's list of least favorite journalists."[6] Interviewed by Boehlert, Suskind argued that these practices represented a break with "a long and venerable tradition in this country." Asked if these attacks on the press were designed to do away with investigative journalism, he replied:

Absolutely. That's the whole idea, to sweep away the community of honest brokers in America—both Republicans and Democrats and members of the mainstream press—sweep them away so we'll be left with a culture and public dialogue based on assertion rather than authenticity, on claim rather than fact. Because when you arrive at that place, then all you have to rely on is perception. And perception as the handmaiden of forceful executive power is the great combination that we're seeing now in the American polity.[7]

Paradoxically, it was the far-right commentator Pat Buchanan's magazine *The American Conservative* which asked, with a certain lucidity:

How did realism become a submerged, almost dissident philosophy amongst American elites, and how did its opposite triumph so completely? Unless one chalks it up simply to the historical caprice of the Bush presidency combined with 9/11, one must consider the motivations of major donors and the myriad factors that determine the acceptable limits of what people in think tanks think. If powerful Americans think differently about the world than they did in the late 1940s and 1950s, an explanation should be sought.[8]

From Propaganda to Infotainment

The explanation is to be found in American history. The different stages in the history of storytelling and the "fictionalization of history" have been traced in earlier chapters, and their triumph in every domain (marketing, management, the media, political communications) did not emerge *ex nihilo* in the 1990s. They are a logical continuation of a tradition of brainwashing whose foundations were established at the beginning of the twentieth century by American marketing and "propaganda" theorists. While their methods were very similar to their contemporary alter egos who worked in Communist Russia "agit-prop," the way they were deliberately used to promote a cynical capitalism allowed them to be much more effective in the long term.

Even though many other factors were involved, the lasting popularity of a book that is now largely forgotten is symptomatic of this mutation. In his *Propaganda*, Edward Bernays combines the French writer Gustave Le Bon's ideas about crowd psychology with his uncle Sigmund Freud's ideas about the unconscious.[9] He was one of the first to notice how mass brainwashing techniques were to flourish in economic, political, and military communications in the twentieth century. Bernays gives a significant example:

> Czechoslovakia officially became a free state on Monday, October 28, 1918, instead of Sunday, October 27, 1918, because Professor Masaryk realized that the people of the world receive more information and would be more receptive to the announcement of the republic's freedom on a Monday morning than on a Sunday, because the press would have more space to devote to it on Monday morning. Discussing the matter with me before he made the announcement, [President] Professor Masaryk said, "I would be making history for the cables if I changed the date of Czechoslovakia's birth as a free nation." Cables make history and so the date was changed. This incident illustrates the importance of technique in the new propaganda.[10]

In Bernays' view, there was nothing reprehensible about using propaganda: "Let us make haste to put this fine old word back where it belongs, and restore its dignified significance for the use of our children and our children's children."[11] It has to be said that, for Bernays, the word refers to a vast, unexplored field. It would later be referred to as "public relations," and Bernays is regarded as its pioneer.

> Some of the phenomena of this process are criticized—the manipulation of news, the inflation of personality, and the general ballyhoo by which politicians and commercial products and social ideas are brought to the consciousness of the masses. The instruments by which public opinion is organized and focused may be misused. But such organization and focusing are necessary to orderly life.[12]

Throughout the twentieth century, countless works confirmed his cynical observation. In his famous *Rape of the Masses*, Serge Chakotin mentions a book entitled *Feldherr Psychologos* (*Marshall Psychologos*), which was published in Germany in 1922. Its author, Kurt Hesse, was a military man who admired Clausewitz's theses, and it paints a prophetic portrait of a "*Führer*" (according to the author, this was the first time the expression had been used). Marshall Psychologos could compensate for the humiliation of Germany's defeat: "The best quality he has is his speech; it has a full and pure resonance, like a bell, and it reaches the heart of every man ... Often he will play his cards like a gambler, and men will say then that he is a consummate politician. But he alone will know that he is merely playing with human souls as on the strings of a piano."[13]

"Words, Mr. Bond, are the new weapons," claims the press magnate in the film *Tomorrow Never Dies*. Caesar had his legions, and Napoleon had his Grand Army. The magnate has his own divisions: television, the news, magazines. By midnight, he boasts, he will have influenced more people than anyone in history, with the exception of God himself!

There is of course a damning archive of material on propaganda, but restrictions of space mean that it cannot be discussed in any detail here. But, from Edward Louis Bernays to Noam Chomsky and Edward Hermann, from Viktor Klemperer to Jacques Ellul, and, more recently, Philippe Breton, André Schriffin, and Eric Hazan,[14] propaganda has always been seen and criticized as an act, or set of concerted actions, designed to propagate political or ideological contents by using manipulative techniques in various media.[15] Bernays, for example, gives what may now look like a rather quaint list: "The printing press and the newspaper, the railway, the telephone, telegraph, radio and airplanes."[16]

The new electronic media appeared in the 1990s. CNN was no longer the only news channel; it was joined on the cable networks by channels such as Fox News. The Internet became a means of mass communication, and television, which is still Americans' main source of news, was gradually absorbed by industry giants like Disney, Viacom, and Time Warner, which now play a dominant role in packaging news and covering both news stories and scandals. The new rolling news system encourages an anecdotal version of events, a black and white picture of reality, and helps to blur the boundary between reality and fiction more than ever before.

The Bush administration obviously did not invent this new media environment, which is often referred by the neologism "infotainment." But it was the first administration to take office after its appearance, and it made brilliant use of it. *New York Times* op-ed columnist Frank Rich writes:

> The chronicle of how a government told and sold its story is also, inevitably, a chronicle of an American culture that was an all-too-easy mark for the flimflam. The synergistic intersection between that culture and the Bush administration's narrative is a significant piece of the puzzle. Only an overheated 24/7 infotainment culture that had trivialized the very idea of reality (and, with it, what was once known as "news") could be so successfully manipulated by those in power.[17]

Fox News: A Mutation in the History of the Media

"Every morning brings us news from across the globe, yet we are poor in newsworthy stories," wrote Walter Benjamin in 1936. "This is because nowadays no event comes to us without being shot through with explanation. In other words, by now almost nothing happens that benefits storytelling; almost everything benefits information. Actually, it is half the art of storytelling to keep a story free from explanation as one recounts it."[18] Thanks to a strange irony of history, the American channel Fox News seems to have heard Benjamin's complaint: it does keep its stories free from explanation. It replaces actual facts with stories. Almost nothing that is seen in its programming aids understanding, and almost everything promotes an impoverished account of striking events larded with puerile observations.

Fox News was founded in 1996 by the press magnate Rupert Murdoch and Roger Ailes, who was one of Ronald Reagan's first spin doctors (in March 2007, he sparked a lively controversy by intentionally confusing Barack *Obama*, the candidate running for the Democratic primaries, with *Osama* bin Laden). According to the Project for Excellence's 2004 report on the news media, Fox News overtook CNN's audience ratings in 2002. It kept its lead in 2003, gaining over 53 percent of audience ratings and 45 percent of prime-time ratings. During the war in Iraq, its audience ratings shot up and viewing figures for its coverage of the war were higher than CNN's.

Marketing guru Seth Godin has a very clear idea of the reasons behind Fox's success: "Roger Ailes understands that he is in the storytelling business and has used that insight to build a multibillion-dollar business." According to Godin: "The news on television isn't 'true.' It can't be. There's too much to say, too many points of view, too many stories to cover. The best a television journalist can hope to do is combine the crowd-pleasing, ad-selling stories on fires and crime with the insightful but less popular stories on world events. And, we hope, to do it without an obvious bias."[19] Fox News, he goes on, took a different approach:

> Fox knows that this bias exists in any news organization and has decided to use this unavoidable problem to frame the news in a way that matched the worldview of their target audience. What worldviews does this audience share?
> - a desire for a consistent story
> - a point of view that emphasizes personal responsibility, conservative ethics, and Republican politics
> - the appearance of fairness, as opposed to being pandered to...
>
> Every day Fox management sends a memo to all the writers, producers, and on-air talent. The memo outlines the talking points for the day. In other words, it's the story they intend to tell. By managing the news to fit the story (as opposed to the other way around) Fox develops a point of view; it tells a story that viewers are happy to believe. It gives the audience a lie to tell themselves and, just as important, to share.[20]

"We paid $3 billion for these television stations. We will decide what the news is. The news is what we tell you it is!" said David Boylan, head of

Fox Tampa Bay. His comments are reported by Ron Kaufman, who runs the turnoffyourtv.com website. Kaufman goes on: "This, of course, is so far removed from reality that it is risible ... the reporting style is so biased and skewed that trying to find any real information from a news report is quite challenging."[21]

The establishment of Fox News does indeed signal a mutation in the history of the media:

> Instead of its being a random mix of individual biases, Fox News chose to tell a coherent story, a lie that its viewers can choose to believe ... The worldview of the Fox News audience was that they were disrespected by the established media. Suddenly this audience was watching a network that broadcast news that they agreed with. And they were told that they were the mainstream and that the news they were hearing was fair and unbalanced.[22]

The Lie Industry

The success of Fox News and its pseudo-journalism attracted a following in the White House. No longer content with influencing the media or bringing pressure to bear on them, the Bush administration created a truly underground structure by using pubic funds to employ fake journalists to produce and spread false news, reviews, reportages, and investigations. As John S. Carroll, the former editor of the *Los Angeles Times*, explained in a lecture on the ethics of journalism at the University of Oregon in May 2004:

> All across America, there are offices that resemble news rooms, and in those offices there are people who resemble journalists, but they are not engaged in journalism. It is not journalism because it does not regard the reader—or, in the case of broadcasting, the listener or the viewer—as a master to be served. To the contrary, it regards its audience with a cold cynicism. In this realm of pseudo-journalism, the audience is something to be manipulated.[23]

The growing number of local stations provides this propaganda-news with the perfect outlet. The pre-packaged news stories put out by the American administration were manna from heaven for low-budget channels employing very few staff and broadcasting over very wide areas. To mark the first anniversary of 9/11, a Fox News subsidiary broadcast a moving report about how America was helping to liberate women in Afghanistan: the commentary read by journalists working for local stations was part of the package, but the journalists were unaware that the government had written the text. In September 2005, the Government Accountability Office (GAO)—a non-partisan arm of Congress— revealed that the government had engaged in "covert propaganda" by paying conservative commentators to defend its educational policy. [24]

To take another example: on March 14, 2004, a *New York Times* journalist revealed that the Department of Health had paid two fake journalists to defend its policy in two commercials. The advertising campaign cost $124 million, but no mention was made of who had paid for the so-called reports. A government spokesman justified the use of fake news in these terms: "Anyone who has questions about this practice needs to do some research on modern public information campaigns."[25]

More seriously still, Frank Rich reported that in 2006 the GAO revealed that:

> At NASA and NOAA (National Oceanic and Atmospheric Administration), political appointees rewrote or censored public documents and agency press releases if they conveyed scientific findings about pollution and global warming that contradicted administration environmental policies. One NASA appointee even enforced the addition of the word *theory* to any mention of the Big Bang in NASA materials, in keeping with the Christian right's rejection of evolutionary science.[26]

That appointee was forced to resign when the press learned that he had invented his degree in journalism. In his film *An Inconvenient Truth* (2006), Al Gore gives several examples of how the scientific truth was travestied in order to promote the obscurantism of a bygone age.

In July 2007, a former Surgeon General corroborated this analysis in testimony before the House of Representatives. The affair hit the headlines and the *New York Times* reported Richard Carmona as accusing the Bush administration of failing to take scientific criteria into account in its public health decisions. "The administration ... would not allow him to speak or issue reports about stem cells, emergency contraception, sex education, or prison, mental and global health issues."[27] *Le Monde* reported Carmona as saying that: "Anything that did not fit in with the ideological, religious or political programme of those in power was ignored, marginalized or simply buried."[28]

The obscurantism of the fundamentalist Christian right influenced both the Bush administration's reports and the media, which were being asked to rethink the role of journalists and to abandon the investigative journalism that had been so important at the time of Watergate. Journalists were expected to become reporters who were "embedded" in the world according to George W. Bush, which was a virtual world created by the White House's storytellers. At a Bush press conference in February 2005, one Jeff Gannon, speaking of the Democrats, asked the president:

> "How are you going to work with people who seem to have divorced themselves from reality?" Liberal bloggers, their curiosity aroused by such blatant partisanship from a reporter, soon discovered that Gannon wouldn't have known what reality was if it had slapped him in the face. His name was a fake, and he worked for a fake news organization, Talon Web, a Web operation with no known audience and staffed mostly by volunteer Republican activists … The Talon owner, Bobby Eberle, had posted effusive thanks on the Web to both Liddy and Karl Rove for "their assistance, guidance and friendship."[29]

According to Frank Rich, Jeff Gannon regularly attended White House briefings. A careful study of the transcripts of the press conferences reveals that "Jeff" was often called upon to create a diversion when journalists asked embarrassing questions about the Abu Ghraib prison scandal or about Karl Rove's possible involvement in leaking the identity of CIA agent Valerie Plame Wilson.[30] Even the conservative columnist William Safire, who had always supported George W. Bush's policies, stated in September 2005 that "the fundamental right of Americans, through our free press, to penetrate and criticize the workings of our government is under attack as never before."[31]

The manipulation of news also played an essential role in the American occupation of Iraq from 2003 onwards. On December 30, 2005, for instance, the *Los Angeles Times* revealed that the Pentagon had subcontracted the Lincoln Group to publish fake stories for the Iraqi press in order to distract public opinion away from the real situation. The Group was run by a Briton with no experience of communications and a former Marine. "The operation is designed to mask any connection with the US military ... The Lincoln Group's Iraq staff, or its subcontractors, sometimes pose as freelance reporters or advertising executives when they deliver the stories to Baghdad media outlets."[32] The fake stories were reportedly written by members of the American military specializing in "information operations" aimed at the Iraqi press.

Some of the papers labeled the stories as "advertising" to "distinguish them from standard editorial content," but for the most part these "reports," which praised the efforts that the US was making to rebuild the country and denounced the insurgents, were described in the Iraqi press as impartial accounts written by independent journalists.

Several sources confirm that American troops were asked to compose storyboards about events in Iraq. They would describe, for example, a raid by American and Iraqi forces on a supposed insurgent stronghold, or an attack that killed Iraqi citizens. The Lincoln Group helped to translate and place the articles. "One of the military officials said that, as part of a psychological operations campaign that has intensified over the last year, the task force also had purchased an Iraqi newspaper and taken control of a radio station, and was using them to channel pro-American messages to the Iraqi public. Neither is identified as a military mouthpiece."[33]

On November 29, 2005, Defense Secretary Donald Rumsfeld went so far as to claim that: "the proliferation of news organizations in Iraq [was] one of the country's great successes since the ouster of President Saddam Hussein." Besides its contract with the military in Iraq, in 2006 the Lincoln Group won a major contract (up to $100 million over five years) with Special Operations Command, based in Tampa, Florida, to develop a strategic communications campaign in concert with special operations troops stationed around the world.[34]

A Magician at Headquarters

American intervention in Iraq in March 2003 did indeed provide a spectacular illustration of the White House's desire to "create its own reality" by using all the techniques of fictionalization. Anxious not to repeat the mistakes it had made during the first Gulf War of 1991, the

Pentagon paid great attention to its communications strategy. The 500 embedded journalists have been widely mentioned, and a great deal of care went into designing the press room in the US forces' headquarters in Qatar. A storage hangar was reconfigured—at the modest cost of one billion dollars—as an ultramodern TV studio, complete with podium, plasma screens, and a whole electronic arsenal capable of producing real-time combat videos, geographical charts, animated films, and diagrams.

The stage on which US Army spokesman Tommy Franks was to address the press was created by a designer who had worked for Disney, MGM, and TV's *Good Morning America*. Since 2001, he had been employed by the White House to design backdrops for the president's appearances, but there is nothing surprising about that, given the links between the Pentagon and Hollywood. What was more surprising was the Pentagon's decision to recruit David Blaine to work on the conversion. Blaine is a magician famous in the US for his TV show and the conjuring tricks that allow him to defy the laws of physics by levitating himself or going without food for days while shut in a cage—not that the two are incompatible. In a book published in 2002,[35] Blaine described himself as the "Michael Jordan of magic" and claimed to be the heir to Robert-Houdin, the legendary French conjurer who, in the nineteenth century, agreed to go to Algeria on the government's behalf to help put down a rising by demonstrating that his magic was more powerful than that of the rebels. Whether or not the Pentagon expected Blaine to do the same is not on record, but it was presumably because his talents as an illusionist could be used to create special effects that he was summoned to the White House and then sent to Qatar.

Not all of this surprising—and highly revelatory—news made it on to the front pages of the American press. It was revealed by Frank Rich, who was for a long time a theater critic, in his 2006 study of the triumph of fiction in the management of public affairs. The book, which has already been cited, is subtitled "The Decline and Fall of Truth in Bush's America." Not the least of this enchanted world's paradoxes is that it was a theater critic who did so much to help unmask it. Discussing Rich's book in the *New York Review of Books* in 2007, Michael Tomasky commented:

Rich is particularly good, in fact, on the question of sets and back-drops, which in its early days the Bush administration used to such Napoleonic effect to lead television viewers toward the desired conclusion. Rich documents the way that Scott Sforza, a former ABC producer who worked for the Republican propaganda machine, created many of the backdrops against which Bush delivered key speeches. It took a special sort of chutzpah in the summer of 2002, during the Enron, Tyco, WorldCom, and other scandals, to push Bush in front of a backdrop that said, over and over, "Corporate Responsibility," or one, at an economic forum in Waco, Texas, that repeated the phrase "Strengthening our economy."[36]

It was Sforza who stage-managed Bush's speech of May 1, 2003, on board the aircraft carrier *Abraham Lincoln*. Speaking in front of a banner emblazoned with the slogan "Mission Accomplished," he solemnly announced: "Major combat operations in Iraq have ended. In the battle of Iraq, the United States and our allies have prevailed." The stage-management did not end there. The president landed on the carrier in a fighter that had been renamed "Navy One" for the occasion; it bore the inscription "George Bush, Commander in Chief." He climbed out of the cockpit, draped in combat gear and helmet in hand, as though he had just returned from a mission in some stunning remake of *Top Gun*. That film was produced by Jerry Bruckheimer, who is very familiar with Holly-wood–Pentagon joint operations and who produced a reality TV show about the war in Afghanistan called *Profiles from the Front Line*. Frank Rich reports how the Fox News's pundit remarked that "This was fantastic theater." He meant it as a compliment. The *Washington Post*'s David Broder was "agog" over what he called the president's "physical posture."[37] Sforza had carefully ensured that the camera angle did not reveal the San Diego skyline less than 40 miles away; the aircraft carrier was supposed to be on the high seas in the combat zone.

But no presidential speech has ever been more stage-managed than that of August 15, 2002, when Bush solemnly spoke about "national security" at Mount Rushmore, where the faces of Washington, Jefferson, Roosevelt, and Lincoln are carved in the rock. During his speech, the cameras were positioned so that Bush was seen in profile, with his face superimposed on those of his famous predecessors.

Three weeks later, recounts Rich, Bush spoke on the first anniversary of 9/11 in order to prepare public opinion for the invasion of Iraq, "the great struggle that tests our strength, and even more so our resolve." Sforza hired three barges to ferry the presidential entourage to the foot of the Statue of Liberty, which he had lit from below with powerful lights. The camera angles were chosen to ensure that the statue served as a backdrop to the president's speech. Rich cites the specialist Michael Deever, the impresario of Ronald Reagan's 1980 presidential announcement speech, with its own Statue of Liberty backdrop: "They understand the visuals as well as anybody ever has … They understand that what's around the head is just as important as the head."[38]

It is "what's around the head" that transforms an image into a legend: "Mission Accomplished," the founding fathers, the Statue of Liberty… This is iconography for beginners. Inscribed in time, the image becomes a story. But it also has to resonate with the viewer, or in other words establish a dialogue between two moments in history: the moment represented in the image and the real moment of its reception. That is what produces the emotion. Frank Rich calls it "timing": "Timing, being everything, was at least as important as the visuals. For Americans in 2002, no date could lend more emotional weight to a speech about war than the first anniversary of 9/11. And besides, the country was just back from vacation, ready to focus on big-ticket items."[39]

When asked about the choice of date, White House chief of staff Andrew Card did not in fact use that argument; he was much more prosaic: "From a marketing point of view, you don't introduce new products in August."

From Uncle Ben's to Uncle Sam

The American state's use of storytelling techniques was obviously not restricted to the White House during the "Bush Jr. years." As early as 1998, a US Air Force manual on "Psychological Operations" (psych-ops) claimed that:

> There is a growing information infrastructure that transcends industry, the media, and the military, and includes both government and non-government entities. It is characterized by a merging of civilian and military information networks and technologies … In this environment psych-ops are "designed to convey selected information and

indicators to foreign traders and audiences to influence their emotions, motives, objective reasoning, and ultimately their behaviour."[40]

As the political scientist Nancy Snow, a professor at California State University, recalls, when Colin Powell was appointed Secretary of State in March 2001, he said: "I'm going to be bringing in people into the public diplomacy function of the department who are going to really ... branding foreign policy, branding the department, marketing American values to the world."[41]

Three weeks after 9/11, Charlotte Beers was appointed Under-Secretary for Public Diplomacy and Public Affairs. During the 1990s, she ran J. Walter Thompson and Ogilvy & Mather, two of America's biggest advertising agencies. This was the first time that a marketing professional had been appointed to a post with diplomatic responsibilities and not just to an advisory post. In an interview with Beers on *Good Morning America*, anchorwoman Diane Sawyer described her as "the woman whose job it is to tell the world who America is and make the Muslim world understand. Talk about a daunting assignment." [42]

In the course of the interview, Beers explained that she wanted to use the resources of the Department of State's website—one of the most sophisticated in the world—to apply marketing techniques to modern diplomacy, because diplomacy was no longer simply a matter of communicating rationally with governments and elites. It had to market emotions if it wanted to communicate with mass markets around the world: "This is not a reasonable argument we're engaged in; it includes some emotions."

In 1999, the *Financial Times* introduced Charlotte Beers by explaining that she had three obsessions—branding, branding, and branding—and "never stopped talking about it." She had no political experience, but she did have a solid background in marketing. The woman known as "the steel magnolia of advertising" was "immediately thrust into the media spotlight as head of the administration's new war on terrorism." *Advertising Age* joked that "The State Department which implemented the Monroe doctrine is about to embrace a new doctrine: branding."[43]

When challenged about her appointment, Colin Powell had to defend his decision to members of Congress: "Guess what? She got me to buy Uncle Ben's rice. So there is nothing wrong with getting somebody who knows how to sell something." The press had a field day with this. She had succeeded in selling the Uncle Ben's brand to Colin Powell, but could she sell Uncle Sam to the rest of the world? (Beers herself admitted that: "This is the most sophisticated brand assignment I've ever had.")[44]

According to Charlotte Beers, the Internet explosion had changed the face of political communications:

> People who have a story to tell, however negative or terrorist [*sic*], are emboldened by the possibilities of doing mass communications ... And that also includes a very one-dimensional picture of America. So what we have to do is persuade our Congress and our constituencies everywhere in the world that we have to answer this and we have to get into young people's hearts and minds. We have to broaden these audiences past the elite and governments ... And we have to activate every single person who can speak well on behalf of the United States.[45]

She in fact played the role of a real Secretary for Propaganda, "with emphasis on developing strategies and programs for communicating with Arab and Muslim audiences around the world."[46] For two years, she devoted herself to applying the techniques of branding and storytelling to foreign policy, and to using brochures, commercials and videos to popularize the administration's version of American values and virtues. She was behind the creation of Radio Free Afghanistan, and at her suggestion the State Department put a few pages online about the lives of Muslims in the United States, complete with stories about happy families and pictures of American mosques. In March 2003, she resigned from her post.

As Nancy Snow wrote: "Madison Avenue, Hollywood and the White House must do their triad campaign, but their storytelling will always be somewhat suspect as manufactured spin that promotes a particular United States policy ... The world continues to view us predominantly as a product, not as a country of diverse peoples with dissenting principles."[47]

At a press briefing on December 18, 2002, a few months before the start of the war in Iraq, "State Department public diplomacy chief Charlotte Beers extolled the importance of 'storytelling' in convincing overseas audiences that the US is only trying to do good." She cited George W. Bush's remarks in *From Fear to Freedom*, which was published by the State Department: "I hope the people of Iraq will remember our history. America has never sought to dominate, never sought to conquer. We have, in fact, sought to liberate and free. Our desire is to help Iraqi citizens find the blessings of liberty within their own culture and their own traditions."

Beers explained:

"And that's something we really have to get better at. This is an emotionally laden universe now. It's not just the facts that are operating in the world now. It's also something as emotional as terrorists, and violence, and religion, and spiritual issues. So, often now, we turn not just to the facts or the words or even the speaker on camera, but to books and pictures and something that conveys stories." Several protesters began shouting "You're selling war and we're not buying."[48]

Storytelling as Propaganda

Two years after his article, Ron Suskind admitted he "didn't fully comprehend" that Bush's aide's comments about the reality-based community got "to the heart of the Bush presidency." Eric Boehlert commented that Suskind's article demonstrated "the extent and degree to which Bush and his senior aides are 'faith-based' in their decision-making, and disdain those who are 'reality-based'. It also discusses how Bush allegedly sends special symbolic signals to his evangelical constituency of 'faith-based' true believers."[49]

The Bush administration's propaganda was amplified by publicity campaigns orchestrated by the Christian right and conservatives:

Christian bloggers are part of a growing group of Christian news providers. The Christian Broadcasting Network, home to Pat Robertson's *700 Clubs*, employs more than one thousand people ... Evangelicals control six national TV networks and over two thousand religious stations ... This well-funded network includes newsletters, think tanks and talk radio as well as cable television news and the Internet. Often in cooperation with the White House, these outlets have launched a systematic campaign to discredit what they refer to disparagingly as "MSM," for mainstream media.[50]

The French philosopher Jean Lacroix seems to have foreseen this development in 1946. Writing in the journal *Esprit*, he remarked that: "Propaganda is not just brainwashing. Truly democratic propaganda does not necessarily go downwards from the government to those who are governed, or from state to nation. It is in fact an expression of the active involvement of the masses in the democratic life of the nation through actions and attitudes."[51] We now know—and this, perhaps, is the Bush administration's greatest contribution to the recent history of propaganda—that this transversal propaganda does not rule out top-down brainwashing, unless it can be described as progressive ... assuming that we are subscribe to Chesterton's aphorism to the effect that "Apparently, progress means being moved along—by the police."

In his *Propaganda*, Edward Bernays reminds us that the *Standard Dictionary* tells us that "The word was applied to a congregation or society of cardinals for the care and oversight of foreign missions which was instituted at Rome in the year 1627. It was also applied to the College of Propaganda at Rome founded by Pope Urban VIII, for the education of the missionary priests. Hence, in later years, the term came to be applied to any institution or scheme for propagating a doctrine or system."[52] The word "propaganda" comes from the Latin; the gerundive form refers to that element of faith that must be *propagated*: beliefs, mysteries, the legends of the saints, stories of miracles. It is therefore not a matter of spreading objective knowledge that is rationally available to all, but of converting people to hidden truths that are a question of faith and not reason.

The Bush administration's use of propaganda therefore constitutes a sort of return to the word's etymological origins. Propaganda must not simply modify or influence individuals' opinions: it must influence all their beliefs and their *habitus*: culture, ideology, and religion. Influencing individual consciousnesses gives way to the interactive and social propagation of a form of belief. George W. Bush happily described it as a "crusade."

"Fire in the Mind"

In his second inaugural address of January 20, 2005, Bush celebrated his "democratic" crusade thus: "By our efforts, we have lit a fire—a fire in the hearts of men. It warms those who feel its power, it burns those who fight its progress, and one day this fire will reach the darkest corners of our world."[53] He presumably did not know that the phrase, which was suggested to him by Karl Rove, comes, as Slavoj Žižek notes, from Dostoyevsky's novel *The Possessed*, where it refers to "the ruthless activity of radical anarchists who burned a village: 'The fire is in the minds of men, not on the roofs of houses.'"[54]

The quotation from Dostoyevsky was probably not something that Karl Rove remembered from school. *Fire in the Minds of Men* is also the title of an essay by the American political scientist and historian James H. Billington, which had been published twenty-five years earlier by the neoconservative Basic Books. The book, which looks at the origins of the French and Russian revolutions, concludes that the revolutionary idea is *religious*: "Modern revolutionaries are believers, no less committed and intense than were the Christians or Muslims of an earlier era. [This revolutionary faith] is perhaps *the* faith of our times."[55]

"Today, again, the world narrative belongs to terrorists," Don DeLillo wrote in *Harper's Magazine* after 9/11.[56] Taken out of context, his formulation may seem ambiguous, but it does not mean that the dominant narrative is that of the terrorists. It means that the world narrative itself has become terroristic. It is a regime of fiction and terror, and it is inscribed within a symbolic field where terrorist-inspired representations and counter-representations clash. The American sociologist Jeffrey C. Alexander is saying exactly the same when he asserts that "We need to theorize terrorism … as a particularly gruesome kind of symbolic action in a complex performative field … [and] the American response to that terror [as] a counter-performance that continues to structure the cultural pragmatics of national and international politics today."[57]

This analysis defies common sense. Common sense would have it that the decisions made by states, including the United States of America, obey only the logic of strictly rational interests (increasing the profits of American multinationals, securing the country's hydrocarbon supplies, and so on). The pursuit of those objectives is, however, by no means in conflict with the pragmatics of symbolic actions that take the form of what Peter Sloterdijk calls "thematic epidemics,"[58] the only difference being that it is not themes that spread, but useful narratives and effective emotions subject to the effects of the mimetic contagion (or contagious seduction) that Gabriel Tarde described as a "current of imitations."[59] As the American management consultant Lori Silverman puts it, it is now "stories that are 'like viruses.' They are contagious."[60]

Thanks to the extension of the Internet, cable television, and the increase in the number of blogs, which have become so many relays for viral marketing, these imitative mechanisms are now reinforced by new and reticular forms of communication. Propaganda action therefore no longer targets socio-professional categories, market shares, or segments of the population, but highly contagious places and milieus. In the United States, faith-based communities have become real sources of contagion that spread viral communications by using the new interactive technologies.

When he evoked the fires lit by Russian nihilists, Karl Rove applied Billington's messianic analysis quite literally: if revolutionaries are believers and if revolutionary faith is the faith of our times, then the faith of the neoconservatives can be revolutionary, and it can reconfigure and convert the real world. That is the real meaning of the American conservative revolution and its faith-based narrative. We thought that the neoconservatives were fighting the "nihilists," but we have caught them *in flagrante*: they are guilty of creating legends, and they are trapped in their metaphors. And their narratives are borrowed: the fire really is in the minds of men and not on the roofs of houses...

Afterword: Obama in Fabula

At the beginning of 2008, the BBC's Washington correspondent Katty Kay remarked that the United States was "like a giant book club." Americans voted for their favorite literary genre and could choose between Barack's ballads, Huckabee's haikus, Rudy [Giuliani]'s rap, Hillary's heroic monologues, and so on. And the presidential campaign really did take the form of a competition between narrative genres and not just narratives. And it was the epic that emerged victorious. "Obama's epic wins." That is how the *New York Times* hailed Barack Obama's electoral victory. It was not just an epic or legendary victory, but a victory for the epic genre itself. For the first time, a literary genre was elected by universal suffrage and entered the White House, and its entrance was as unlikely as the sudden appearance of Gogol's "nose" on the streets of St. Petersburg.

Taking her cue from former Governor of New York Mario Cuomo, Hillary Clinton had tried to argue that "You campaign with poetry, but you govern with prose." Her rhetoric was brilliant, but it was out of step with the times. Obama campaigned in prose and not in poetry, and it was a very narrative prose. The first words he uttered on the night of his first victory in Iowa on January 3, 2008, were borrowed from the epic register: "They said this day would never come..." His words echoed Martin Luther King Jr.'s "I have a dream" and sounded like the beginning of a story. It was a story of personal courage and devotion to the nation, a story capable of embodying an individual destiny and inspiring crowds. The aura of predestination surrounding Obama's charismatic personality suddenly crystallized in "this determining moment in history." And when they talked about it, commentators spontaneously adopted the lexicon of revelation, with talk of legendary words, a man of destiny, and a historic election. Obama's sudden appearance in the early stages of the campaign put an end to the chronicle of a nomination foretold—that of Hillary Clinton—and introduced a new narrative tension and heightened the suspense because the outcome was unknown.

Stories Degree Xerox

"The outsized power of the personal narrative today compared with even a generation ago ... reflects something that has become a cliché in political analysis," observes *Newsweek*'s Sharon Begley. "Emotions, more than a dispassionate and rational analysis of candidates' records and positions, determine many voters' choice on election day." She cites the famous neuroscientist Antonio Damasio as saying that, when Roosevelt was making radio addresses, "people had the time needed for reflection, to mix emotion with facts and reason. But now, with 24-hour cable news and the Web, you have a climate in which you don't have time to reflect ... Voters are being driven by pure like and dislike, comfort or discomfort with a personality ... And voters judge that by a candidate's narrative."[1]

Novelists know all about feelings of like or dislike, and comfort or discomfort. These are the feelings they inspire in their readers. If the novel works, the feelings associated with this or that character change from one situation to the next, and they come into conflict or are reconciled, but they always find their place in a reconstructed narrative order with which the reader can empathize. Ultimately, that empathy works to the advantage of the narrator by giving him or her credibility.

The credibility of the narrator is therefore the key to a narrative's performativity, both in literature and in politics. But while credibility is, in literary terms, a reading-effect, the credibility of a narrator who is involved in an election campaign is constantly under threat and can be destroyed by a rumor or calumny. The Democratic primaries were the theater for competing narratives.

Jean Baudrillard would have greatly enjoyed the "Warholian" moment in the campaign when Hillary Clinton, who was doing badly in the polls, described Obama's proposals for change as a Xerox copy: "If your candidacy is going to be about words, they should be your words. Lifting whole passages is not change you can believe in, it's change you can Xerox."

The accusation of plagiarism marked an escalation in the attempt to deny the legitimacy of the Democratic candidate. It was not aimed at the

candidate's life or personality, his human qualities or his political expertise. There were no revelations about his conduct during the war in
Vietnam (Kerry), his sexual peccadilloes (Clinton), his alcoholism
(Bush), or any other episode in his biography. But doubt was cast on his
ability to tell stories and his credibility as a storyteller.

The argument was, at bottom, specious, as Obama was one of the few
candidates in American political history to write his own speeches. That,
however, was not the point. "That's the difference between my
Democratic opponent and me," declared Clinton. "I offer solutions." In
reply, Obama treated her to a lesson in rhetoric: "Don't tell me words
don't count. 'I have a dream.' Just words. 'We hold these truths to be
self-evident, that all men are created equal.' Just words. 'We have
nothing to fear but fear itself.' Just words. Just speeches."

Was the Democratic primary a contest between two visions of campaigning, one based upon programs and actions, and the other of dreams
and words? Was one waged "with prose," and one "with poetry," as
Hillary Clinton put it? What better story could there be than that of the
return of the Clintons to the White House after George W. Bush's two
terms in office? That would have been a story about nostalgia for the
1990s and, for the American middle classes, it would have been about the
return of peace and prosperity. But it reckoned without Obama's story,
which would contrast nostalgia for the Clinton era with the aspiration
towards change and celebrate the "rainbow" story of reconciliation that
could unite a divided America. One nation. One narration. So what was
the point of contrasting experience with change, concrete projects with
vague promises, the real with the virtual, and actions with words, when
Obama's campaign drew its strength from a story about change incar-
nate, or in other words from both a promise and a plot? In performative
terms, the only way to ruin Obama's story was to undermine his credibility as a storyteller. This is an old criticism that has often been addressed
to postcolonial writers and hybrid literatures; it raises doubts about the
authenticity of the texts, but it also queries whether "ex-colonials" can
have an "original" and "authentic" identity. If you did not write these
speeches, then who inspired them? Who the hell wrote them? Why
should we believe these fine stories, even if they are charming? It was
insinuated that Senator Obama's candidacy was based on the strength of
his rhetoric and promises, but that he did not keep his promises and that
his rhetoric was not his own.

Political campaigns now take place in a performative space in which stories matter more than political programs, and in which the qualities required of a candidate have been displaced from the administrative, juridical, economic, or ethical field towards that of rhetoric. Political skills have given way to fictional competence, and presidential legitimacy to the credibility of a storyteller. And that credibility is acquired not only by making speeches, but from electoral combat, which now takes the form of verbal jousting and challenges.

Hillary Clinton's Cojones

Once Hillary Clinton's advisers had distilled doubts about the authenticity of Obama's speeches about change, the Clinton clan tried to cast aspersions on his virility. Had he more or less *cojones* than Hillary, a woman who does, as her most fervent supporters tell us, have them? Despite its apparent vulgarity, the affair deserves our attention. James Carville was so bold as to tell *Newsweek* that "If she gave him one of her *cojones*, they'd both have two."[2] Whilst it betrays a certain desperation, the attack is not as far-fetched as it might seem. Bush's America had become accustomed to martial posturing, and perhaps the election would be decided by the candidate's *habitus*. Would he be a fighter or a negotiator? A dreamer or a macho man? At a meeting in New York, and in the presence of the senator, union boss Paul Gibson described Clinton as having "testicular fortitude." This is a form of competition that not even Lewis Carroll could have imagined, even though he dreamed up the memorably absurd "caucus race": the *cojones* caucus. *New York Times* op-ed columnist Maureen Dowd asked "¿Quién es less macho?"[3] and the *Guardian's* Nicholas Mills described the primaries in North Carolina and Indiana as "the testosterone primaries."[4] Mike Easley, the governor of North Carolina—a state that was eventually won by Barack Obama—justified his support for Clinton by comparing her with Rocky Balboa, the boxer played by Sylvester Stallone: "She makes Rocky Balboa look like a pansy. There is nothing I like more than a strong powerful woman."[5]

We know that "sex" and "gender" are two different things. "Femininity" and "virility" are not so much "biological characteristics" of the two sexes as socially constructed "markers." But perhaps not sufficient emphasis has been placed on the extent to which these characteristics have become unstable in the era of what Judith Butler calls the "politics of the performative." They are displaced by the performance of those who choose them. If we look at the two Democratic candidates, we find that the sexual "poles" have been reversed to a certain extent. The female candidate played on the signs of virility, if not machismo: expertise, competence, experience, endurance, rationality ... while the man displayed signs that tend to be associated with the "female" pole: charisma or even charm, the values of dialogue and compromise rather than those of confrontation, the promise of change rather than the lessons of experience, hope rather than expertise, elegance rather than endurance, and, as Hillary complained, the lyricism of campaigning rather than the prose of good governance.

Sister Sarah and Sexy Palin

Norman Mailer said of the 1960 Democratic convention, which endorsed John F. Kennedy as the party's candidate, that it "began as one mystery and ended as another."[6] The same could be said of the 2008 Republican convention, the only difference being that it began with a hurricane and ended with an apparition. The apparition was Sarah Palin, who came from the far North with her Down syndrome baby and her pregnant daughter to redeem America. In 1960, Mailer analyzed the American soul, which was, in his view, typified by the "double life" his fellow citizens had been leading since the First World War. Their real, concrete political life was fact-based and incredibly boring, but there was also "the second American life, the long electric night with the fires of neon leading down the highway to the murmur of jazz." Mailer summed up the situation thus: "mysteries are irritated by facts." After George W. Bush's two terms in office, the American imaginary's combination of ecstasy and violence had reached such a degree of concentration that it made possible a phenomenon as unlikely as Sarah Palin's sudden appearance on the political scene. The press laughed at her lack of preparation, but it did make her stand out from the professional politicians from Washington. The McCain team was criticized for the inadequacies of its vetting procedures, but miracles do not need to be vetted. And Sarah Palin was either a (media) miracle or, which boils down to the same thing, a dramatic persona.

Being an expert on such things, Barack Obama immediately identified the nature of the "phenomenon" when he said: "Palin is a great story." Being a story means displaying all the signs of the fable.

As Joe Klein pointed out in *Time* magazine, Sarah Palin could be seen as a new incarnation of the old Reagan-style myth of small-town America and represented the brave, honest heroes "who do some of the hardest work in America, who grow our food and fight our wars."[7] But Sarah Palin also had other cards up her sleeve. She was a composite figure who could reflect the myriad facets of a volatile and scattered electorate. She embodied conservatism and change, religion and marketing. She was both a mother and a liberated woman. Sarah hit the headlines, and that is what she was asked to do by her reader-voters: "Astonish me! Give me suspense and a plot." The lesson of this campaign was, as David Brooks wrote in the *New York Times*, that "weirdness wins." And Palin was weird. Like any star of a reality TV show, she was as transgressive as anyone could wish. She was intriguing and disturbing. She was the source of scandals and polemics, and as much a "buzz-maker" as a "myth-maker." She "electrifies the GOP and galvanizes the twitterati," wrote *Wired* magazine.[8] She was a mother, and she was sexy. A macho mama. Sister Sarah and Sexy Palin. "Here was McCain, the angry old warrior, deploying sex as a central political weapon to recharge his potency," wrote Joann Wypijewski in *The Nation*.[9] The Republicans had not chosen just any woman to win over women voters who had been disappointed by Hillary Clinton's withdrawal from the campaign. They had chosen a woman who was also a sex symbol. Ever since their anti-gay crusade, Christian fundamentalists had learned throughout the 1970s to use the sex weapon on behalf of the heterosexual family. They held out "mind-blowing sex as God's special gift," and this was, according to Wypijewski, a godsend for "a multimillion dollar industry in Christian sex guides, aids, toys, soft-core porn ... promoting a particular image of married women as sex machine." Never before had the construction of a major political figure or the image of a mother been so closely associated with pornographic fantasies. Rush Limbaugh, a radio broadcaster with one of the biggest audiences in the country, was one of the first to encourage Palin to run in February. He could not hide his satisfaction: "Sarah Palin, babies, guns, Jesus. Hot damn!"

Obama's Magic Square

"This is the only time to compare the two candidates side by side," noted David Axelrod on the eve of the final debate in the campaign, which would confirm what had become apparent in previous debates: Obama's strategy was one of differentiation rather than confrontation. And the distance between the two candidates for the presidency of the United States had never looked greater. The difference was of course stylistic as well as generational. But the difference between the candidates' political "age" was much more important than their biological age difference. They stood on opposite sides of a divide that could not be measured purely in terms of years. Two Americas and two worlds were staring at one another in incredulity, and one of them was on its way out. McCain belonged to the Gutenberg galaxy, and his heroes, like those of the Hemingway he admired, were of pen and ink, and hewn from the marble of lived experience. They were rugged and stony. Obama was from Planet Internet. He was a man on the move and a man with multiple loyalties. He was a "liquid" hero, and still in the process of evolving. Elegance and eloquence were not his only trump cards. He owed his victory to a war machine that could be defined as a new model for campaigning. Like the four sides of a magic square, it combined four functions:

- Tell a story that can construct the candidate's narrative identity (storyline).
- Make history an integral part of the campaign, manage its rhythms and its narrative tension throughout the campaign (timing).
- Frame the candidate's ideological message, or in other words frame the debate, as recommended by the linguist Georges Lakoff, by using a "coherent register of language" and "creating metaphors" (framing).
- Create the network on the Internet and on the ground, or in other words create a hybrid and contagious environment that can capture the attention of the candidate's audience and structure that audience (networking).

Obama and McCain drew over the first point. Both had written memoirs, and their titles (*Faith of My Fathers*, *Dreams from My Father*) winked at each other ironically. The candidates' stories had become key elements in their election campaigns. Every episode in the life of a candidate is the narrative atom of a political identity. A presidential character is a narrative personified, and a performer. Political conventions are his stage. The same was true of McCain, but it was in Denver that this became really obvious. "All the speeches seem to have been written by the same storyteller," remarked *Le Monde*'s correspondent Corinne Lesnes with some irony. Barack Obama's half-sister Maya Soetero-Ng talked about their mother, who was a storyteller. His wife Michelle made the story of their two families part of the family saga of middle-class America: "Isn't this an American Story?" And the Kennedy dynasty's last survivor handed on the torch of the presidential legend.

At every other level (timing, framing, and networking), the Obama campaign enjoyed a crushing superiority. McCain constantly mistimed things, suspended his campaign twice, and tried to distract voters' attention by launching defamatory attacks on his rival. Torn between his persona as the one man who could save the Republican party (the famous maverick with a "moderate" line on moral issues) and his choice of the ultra-conservative Sarah Palin as a running mate, he contradicted himself. His program fell apart and left him looking like a candidate in search of a definition. By contrast, the eruption of the financial crisis fitted in remarkably well with Obama's agenda because it created a horizon of expectations: regulatory interventionism and a social and fiscal policy that would favor the middle classes. From the Iowa primaries onwards, Obama successfully made his personal history an integral part of the campaign and transformed the contest with Hillary Clinton into a heroic journey in search of America. The contest was staged at the Denver convention. It was a theater of the third kind and addressed three audiences simultaneously: a crowd of 80,000 people, plus television viewers and net surfers. Thanks to a clever backdrop simulating the front of the White House, the event's stage designer succeeded in fusing two very different types of performance. This was both a happening and an episode from a TV series, Woodstock and *The West Wing*. Barack Obama was the embodiment of both the function of the president and a presidential fiction.

Blogger Andrew Sullivan praised his mastery of the "Facebook politics," and in the *New York Times* Roger Cohen compared the Obama campaign's rise to power with the now classic success of the "Internet start-ups." The Internet campaign encouraged mass participation and gradually spread messages and stories about the candidate through a nebula of wiki-activists, digital campaign pioneers, MySpace activists, Twitterati, and YouTubers. They were the miracle workers—and it was a miracle—who won over more donors and sponsors. Roosevelt was a president for the radio age, and Kennedy a president for the television age: was Obama to become the first elected president of the digital age?

Politics' "Second Life"

One of the clichés of this presidential campaign was that political life was becoming more and more "fictionalized" because there were so many similarities between the ups and downs of the campaign and TV series such as *The West Wing*.

Obama's destiny did indeed seem to owe everything to the series in which, contrary to all expectations, the Hispanic candidate Matt Santos is elected to the presidency of the United States. Matt Santos began his career as a community organizer. He is married with two children. At a Democratic convention he defeated the party machine supporting the candidacy of the vice-president. His rivals attacked him because of his lack of political experience, and he responded with great speeches inspired by national reconciliation and change.

How are we to analyze these similarities between fiction and reality? Who is imitating whom, the fictional candidate or the fictional hero? Was Obama's destiny straight out of a Hollywood screenplay designed to restore America's luster? The idea is attractive, but it is wrong. In an interview with the *Guardian*, scriptwriter and producer Eli Attie revealed that the model he had used to construct the Santos character was ... Barack Obama! Impressed by his speech at the 2004 Democratic convention, Attie had called David Axelrod to find out more about the young senator from Illinois. Santos was no less than Obama's fictional double.

Within a few months, *The West Wing* became the real prism through which the campaign was viewed. It was both the bible for commentators, and a *vade mecum* for politicians lost in the mediasphere. *The West Wing* was not just a cult series praised for its intelligence and educational value; it was also the site and instrument that collapsed fiction and reality. The countless similarities between the candidates' biographies, right down to their age and skin color, were designed to convince us that there is no alternative to the fictionalization of politics. Bill Clinton's former press secretary Dee Dee Myers, who became a consultant on the series, admitted that "the script bulged with real life plots taken directly from the experience of the Clinton White House." Some Clinton aides who never had access to the Oval Office had themselves photographed in the *West Wing* studios. In an e-mail to Elie Attie, David Axelrod wrote, "We're living your scripts."[10] McCain reportedly recognized himself in his fictional double Arnold Vinick, a seventy-year-old, non-conformist, divorced "maverick" who does not adopt his party's "faith-based" positions on social issues. Some fans actually came to see the McCain/Obama duel as a pale reflection of the one between their fictional doubles Matt Santos and Arnold Vinick. The series *K Street* brought this confusion between reality and fiction to the screen by using both actors and real figures such as James Carville and Howard Dean, who was a candidate for the 2004 Democratic primaries. In the early stages of the campaign, Dean used a line suggested to him by his coaches in one episode of the series. We see the real James Carville following the real debate on television, and we hear Howard Dean using a line that had featured in an earlier episode. At this point, the circle was unbroken. This was complete simulation. Increasingly, political events seemed to have been scripted in advance, doubles of their own screenplays. The reason why this reflects our distinction between "reality" and "fiction" so well is that they are both part of the same world in which real experience has given way to simulation protocols as stories inject a simulated reality, or serialized story-experiences, into everything. This is democracy's spectral second life. This is the "Second Life" of politics.

Obama's Narrator

Obama's success inspired a lot of imitators. David Axelrod's "ethical" storytelling will surely have as many followers as Karl Rove's "cynical" storytelling. Axelrod has been described as Obama's Karl Rove ever since the Iowa caucus.[11] That makes Axelrod laugh, and he rejects the comparison because the way he sees his role is quite the opposite of the Scheherazade strategy Rove adopted during both Bush's terms in office.

In his view, the world of political consultancy suffers from a "Wizard of Oz strategy": consultants try to get their candidate elected by giving him an artificial story and asking him to conform to it. He knew his job, he said, and was familiar with political techniques such as polls and focus groups. He accepted that everything they did in a way contributed to an atmosphere of cynicism and claimed to be trying to put an end to that. He takes the view that this lack of authenticity explains the Democrats' failure in recent presidential elections.

The *Washington Post*'s correspondent Howard Kurtz observed that the journalists covering Obama's campaign were astonished that they were not being given any particular attention from the usual spin doctors, who try to use analyses and commentaries to influence the press: "The contrast in his press campaign is striking, not just with Clinton's campaign—but also with the Bush White House and the Clinton White House before that. The Obama campaign is a bit of an odd duck. 'There is no charm offensive towards the Press,' said *Newsweek*'s correspondent Richard Wolffe. 'The contact is limited. They see the national media more as a logistical problem than as a channel for getting stuff out.' "[12] The linguist George Lakoff, founder of the Rockridge Institute think tank which tries to help the Democrats to frame their message, regards Barack Obama as his best pupil. Asked about his influence, Obama replied: "You know, I love Lakoff. I think he's an insightful guy. But the fact is I am not a propagandist. That's not my job."[13]

Throughout his campaign, Obama denounced the growing gap between "talk and action," which had been growing wider since the days of Ronald Reagan and "his brand of verbal legerdemain," arguing that it "corrupted both language and thought."[14]

Newly elected to the Senate and under siege from reporters and commentators, he began to ask himself: "How long before the committees of scribes and editors took residence in your head ... How long before you start sounding like a politician?"[15]

There is one Barack Obama who is stubbornly overlooked by the media: the semiologist who pays attention to signs and the way they circulate within the mediasphere. In *The Audacity of Hope*, for instance, he describes how "a particular narrative, repeated over and over and hurled through cyberspace at the speed of light, eventually becomes a hard particle of reality; how political caricatures and nuggets of conventional wisdom lodge themselves in our brain without us ever taking the time to examine them."[16] As he observes, this "rewards not those who are right, but those—like the White House press office—who can make the arguments most loudly, most frequently, most obstinately, and with the best backdrop."[17]

The Politics of Signs

In a public space that is saturated with stories and in which any news item must, if it is to reach its target audience, take the form of a story, the narrative construction of a political identity is no longer left to chance or to the personal talent of the candidate. Books written by candidates serve a specific purpose: every memory, every idea, and every experience is a narrative atom in the sequence that must bring the politician to power. They both program and profile him.

Barack Obama's *Dreams from My Father* reveals a very different relationship with narrative. The book ends at the point when the author is about to begin his studies at Harvard Law School, and had yet to think of making a career in politics. It is both a *Bildungsroman* and a travel book, but it also represents an attempt to deconstruct ready-made stories and myths about childhood: "I learned long ago to distrust my childhood and the stories that shaped it ... many years later ... I understood that I had spent much of my life trying to rewrite these stories, plugging up holes in the narrative, accommodating unwelcome details, projecting individual choices against the blind sweep of history."[18] This is probably the key to his candidacy's appeal to young Americans: his story describes the difficulties of learning about signs and a quest for a hybrid identity as he slipped "back and forth between my black and white worlds, understanding that each possessed its own language and customs and structures of meaning, convinced that with a bit of translation on my part the two worlds would eventually cohere."[19] From a very early age, Obama had to make intensive and careful use of signs: "Since my first frightening discovery of bleaching creams in *Life* magazine, I'd become familiar with the lexicon of color consciousness within the black community—good hair, bad hair, thick lips or thin... You couldn't be sure that everything you had assumed to be an expression of your black, unfettered self—the humor, the song, the behind-the-back pass—had been freely chosen by you. At best, these things were a refuge; at worst, a trap."[20]

David Axelrod has known Obama for 15 years, ever since he was a young community organizer working on a working-class education program in the neighborhoods of Chicago's South Side. He used

Obama's biography to craft a real narrative in which the life of the Democratic candidate and American history merge into one. This complex, polyphonic narrative contrasts sharply with the stereotypical tales of how Bush was saved by his faith. It is full of contrasts and contradictions. It is a faceted mirror in which everyone can recognize themselves: a man from a poor neighborhood and a university graduate, a community organizer and an academic, a realist and an idealist, a man who is willing to compromise and a man who sticks to his principles (on Iraq and torture, for instance). As conservative columnist David Brooks remarked: "He is perpetually engaged in an internal dialogue between different pieces of his hybrid self—Kenya with Harvard, Kansas with the South Side of Chicago—and he takes that conversation outward into the world."[21] He embodies the legend of a global man in the age of globalization. It is his heroic journey that makes his life exemplary: Hawaii, Jakarta, Los Angeles, Chicago, Washington... But it is also a journey through time, punctuated by references to Abraham Lincoln or Martin Luther King Jr., and they make him part of America's history. No matter whether you're a Republican or a Democrat, black or white, man or woman, you are going to elect the first black president of America. That is why the young Obama, criticized by his rivals for his lack of experience, looked from the outset like a "historic" candidate.

A Strategist Appeals to the American Unconscious

After a long campaign across the United States, Obama the storyteller addressed the American people on television one last time and talked about what he had seen during his long months of campaigning: stories of the average America and even, he said, "the stories of the American story." Without renouncing his political, economic, or military responsibilities, the candidate deliberately took on the new function of an executive mandate. His function was part that of a teacher, and part that of a therapist. Like the griots who, in African societies, are described as "doctors of the bond," he both listened to and shared stories. The tone of the story, the way his encounters with the American people were staged, and the iconography of his personal history left no one in any doubt: Dr. Obama had taken upon himself a task that the politicians in Washington seemed to have left to him in despair: curing America of itself. *The Nation* evoked a chronicle of despair—sick people with no health care, retired people forced to work in order to eat, unemployed people hit by the crisis, etc., putting into perspective the woes of an America that had been left to its own devices—and highlighted the candidate's qualities: a willingness to listen, empathy, and energy. This was a story of promise, and a story with biblical overtones.

Obama is much more than a brilliant "storyteller." He is a strategist who appeals to the American unconscious. He has succeeded in turning his hybrid personality, with its heterogeneous points of biographical reference, into a metaphor for the new composite identities of the age of globalization. That is why we should not be analyzing this event in the light of historical analogies (Martin Luther King Jr. or the Kennedys), but in terms of the unprecedented space of the post-9/11 era. Obama holds out to a disoriented America a mirror in which shattered narrative elements can be put together again.

After 9/11, the Republicans inverted America's ideal-types by criminalizing immigration, building border walls, restricting freedom of expression, and over-coding identity in religious terms. Obama has done the opposite. He has replaced the rhetoric of the clash of civilizations with the syntax of assonance and reconciliation, hybrid identities and variations thereon, and an identity that is open to emigrants in an age of displacements. His travels through a hybrid America mark a return to the American story of origins. With Obama, America has found the points of reference it lost after 9/11: immigration, travel, the melting pot, and the frontier as a living and positive dimension. He has made himself the spokesman for "a people already stripped of their history, a people often ill-equipped to retrieve that history in any other form than what fluttered across the television screens."[22]

Beautiful books, wrote Marcel Proust, are written in a sort of foreign language. The same might be said of any form of human expression. And why cannot it be said of political discourse, once it stops mimicking clichés, and begins to use a new language and a new political grammar? The extent of the change can then be measured in terms of the proliferation of new signs, some of them contradictory and some of them convergent, that are difficult to read in the political language of old because they escape the simple message of the communicators and the media logic of persuasion.

The future will tell whether Barack Obama is the inventor of a new political idiom, or merely its simulacrum, a mere "avatar" of Lincoln for the Second Life age. But it would be absurd to deny that he is the embodiment of a new generation of politicians who might be described as semio-politicians, who use signs and symbols rather than programs and promises, and who are less likely to "position" themselves on a traditional spectrum of political forces in order to inspire new ways of thinking about and changing the world.

Notes

Introduction

1 Cited by Sharon Ghamari-Tabrizi, "The Convergence of the Pentagon and Hollywood: The Next Generation of Military Training Simulations," in Lauren Rabinovitz and Abraham Geil, eds, *Memory Bytes: History, Technology, and Digital Culture*, Durham and London: Duke University Press, 2004, p. 151.

2 Cited by Sandy Amerio, *Storytelling: Index sensible pour agora non représentative*, Aubervilliers: Les Laboratoires d'Aubervilliers, 2004.

3 Francesca Polletta, *It Was Like a Fever: Storytelling in Protest and Politics*, Chicago and London: University of Chicago Press, 2006, p. 1.

4 Evan Cornog, *The Power and the Story: How the Crafted Presidential Narrative Has Determined Political Success from George Washington to George W. Bush*, New York: Penguin Press, 2004, pp. 1–2.

5 Gilles Deleuze, "On the Superiority of Anglo-American Literature," in Gilles Deleuze and Claire Parnet, *Dialogues II*, trans. Hugh Tomlinson and Barbara Habberjam, London and New York: Continuum, 2002, p. 27.

6 *Los Angeles Times*, January 11, 2001.

7 Cited by Peter Brooks, "Stories Abounding," *Chronicle of Higher Education*, November 11, 2001.

8 Cited by Matti Hyvärinen, "Towards a Conceptual History of Narrative"; available at www.helsinki.fi

9 Lori Silverman, *Wake Me Up When the Data Is Over*, San Francisco: Jossey-Bass, 2006.

10 Brooks, "Stories Abounding."

11 For the theorists of narrative, this basic distinction overlaps with E. M. Forster's distinction between "story" and "plot," the Russian formalists' distinction between "fable" and "narrative," Benveniste's distinction between *histoire* and *récit*, and Genette's distinction between the diegetic and extra-diegetic levels of narrative discourse. See in particular the three volumes of Gérard Genette's *Figures*, Paris: Seuil, 1966, 1969, 1972; and Jean-Marie Schaeffer, *Pourquoi la fiction?*, Paris: Seuil, 1999.

12 See François Cusset, *French Theory: How Foucault, Derrida, Deleuze, & Co. Transformed the Intellectual Life of the United States*, Minneapolis: University of Minnesota Press, 2008.

13 Roland Barthes, "Introduction to the Structural Analysis of Narrative," in *Image, Music, Text*, trans. Stephen Heath, London: Fontana, 1977, p. 79. (First published as the introductory essay to *Communications* 8, 1966: *Recherches sémiologiques: l'analyse structurale du récit*).

14 Brooks, "Stories Abounding."

15 See my "La Télé-réalité comme laboratoire," in Christian Salmon, *Verbicide: Du Bon Usage des cerveaux humains disponibles*, Arles: Actes Sud, 2007.

16 See Paul Ricoeur, *The Course of Recognition*, trans. David Pellauer, Cambridge, MA: Harvard University Press, 2005.

17 Dominique Christian, *A la recherche du sens dans l'Entreprise... Compter, raconter? La Stratégie du récit*, Paris: Maxima, 1999.

1 From Logo to Story

1 Naomi Klein, *No Logo: Taking Aim at the Brand Bullies*, London: Flamingo, 2000, p. 3.

2 Seth Godin, *All Marketers Are Liars: The Power of Telling Authentic Stories in a Low-Trust World*, New York: Portfolio, 2005, p. 20.

3 Lawrence Vincent, *Legendary Brands: Unleashing the Power of Storytelling to Create a Winning Market Strategy*, Chicago: Dearborn Trade Publishing, 2002, p. 8.

4 Cited in the Techtransform blog, December 7, 2003; www.techtransform.com

5 Klein, *No Logo*, p. 7.

6 Ibid.

7 James Surowiecki, "The Decline of Brands," *Wired*, 12, November 11, 2004.

8 David Foster Wallace, *Infinite Jest*, Boston: Back Bay Books, 1997.

9 Surowiecki, "The Decline of Brands."

10 Ibid.

11 Sophie Peters, "Attention clients, vous êtes observés!", *Les Echos*, September 18, 2006.

12 Cited by Surowiecki, "The Decline of Brands."

13 Rémy Sansaloni, *Le Non-consommateur: Comment le consommateur reprend le pouvoir*, Paris: Dunod, 2006.

14 Al Ries and Laura Ries, *The Fall of Advertising and the Rise of PR*, New York: Harper-Business, 2002, p. xvi.

15 Sergio Zyman, *The End of Advertising As You Know It*, New York: Wiley, 2002, p. 1.

16 Cathy Macherel, "Une Place rebaptisée Nikeplatz à Vienne?," *Le Courrier*, October 31, 2003.

17 Klein, *No Logo*, p. 345.

18 See the Déclaration de Berne's website at www.evb.ch/fr and www.behindthe label.org

19 Cited by Klein, *No Logo*, p. 395.

20 Academics Studying Nike and Athletic and Campus Apparel Industry; see http://business.nmsu.edu

21 Cited by Klein, *No Logo*, p. 189.

22 Cited ibid., p. 345.

23 Cited ibid., p. 189.

24 Kevin Roberts, *Lovemarks: The Future Beyond Brands*, New York: Powerhouse Cultural Entertainment Books, 2004, p. 6.

25 Cited by Klein, *No Logo*, p. 189.

26 Surowiecki, "The Decline of Brands."

27 Karl Marx, *Capital, Vol. I*, trans. Ben Fowkes, Harmondsworth: Penguin, 1976, p. 176.

28 Vincent, *Legendary Brands*, p. 4.

29 Surowiecki, "The Decline of Brands."

30 Sharaf Ramzy and Alicia Korten, "What's In a Name? How Stories Power Enduring Brands," in Lori Silverman, *Wake Me Up When the Data Is Over*, San Francisco: Jossey-Bass, 2006, pp. 170–84.

31 Luc Boltanski and Eve Chiapello, *The New Spirit of Capitalism*, trans. Gregory Elliott, London and New York: Verso, 2005, p. 20.

32 David M. Boje, "Time and Nike," *Time and Nike Symposium*, Academy of Management, Toronto, 2000; available at http://business.nmsu.edu

33 Ashraf and Korten, "What's in a Name?," p. 170.

34 Cited ibid., pp. 172, 175.

35 Cited ibid, pp. 181–2.

36 Stephen Denning, *The Leader's Guide to Storytelling: Mastering the Art and Discipline of Business Narrative*, San Francisco: Jossey-Bass, 2005, p. 105.

37 *L'Entreprise*, 251, December 2006.

38 Cited by David Miller, "Super Bowl Ads Just Won't Let Go," February 3, 2006; available at www.internetnews.com

39 Cited by Ramzy and Korten, "What's in a Name?," p. 182.

40 Cited ibid., pp. 174–5.

41 Peters, "Attention clients, vous êtes observés!"

42 Barbara B. Stern, "What Does Brand Mean?," *Journal of the Academy of Marketing Science*, 34: 2, 2006.

43 Georges M. Hénault, "Les Archétypes jungiens: mythe ou saint Graal du marketing international," *Consommations & Sociétés*, 5, 2005; available at www.argonautes.fr

44 Christian Budtz, Klaus Fog, and Boris Yakabolyu, *Storytelling: Branding in Practice*, New York: Springer, 2005.

45 Godin, *All Marketers Are Liars*, p. 2.

46 Ibid., p. 39.

47 Ibid., p. 2.

48 Ibid., p. 159.

49 Ibid., pp. 163–4.

50 Ibid., p. 159.

51 Vincent, *Legendary Brands*, p. 15.

52 Godin, *All Marketers Are Liars*, p. 17.

53 Ibid., p. 18.

54 Rolf Jensen, *The Dream Society: How the Coming Shift from Information to Imagination Will Transform Your Business*, London: McGraw-Hill, 2001.

55 Cited by Marianne White, "La Vie selon Starck," November 17, 2006; available at www.cyberpresse.ca

56 Georges Lewi, *L'Odyssée des marques*, Paris: Albin Michel, 1998. See also the same author's *Les Marques, mythologies du quotidien*, Paris: Village mondiale, 2003.

57 Scott Rosenberg, "Story Time: Can Narrative Save us from Information Overload?," *Salon*, September 29, 1998; available at http://archive.salon.com

58 Tom Peters, "The Brand Called You," *Fast Company*, August–September 1997.

59 Cited by Klein, *No Logo*, p. 23.

60 Cited by Stephen Denning, "American Brand Narratives in a Post-9/11 World," March 1, 2004; available at www.stevedenning.com

61 Ashraf Ramzy, "The American Story," 2002; available at www.narrativity.net

62 Denning, *The Leader's Guide to Storytelling*, p. xix.

2 The Invention of Storytelling Management

1 Steve Jobs, "You've Got to Find What You Love," Stanford University, 2005; available at http://news-service.stanford.edu/news

2 Howard Bloom, *Reinventing Capitalism: Putting Soul in the Machine. A Radical Reperception of Western Civilization*, 2005; available at www.howardbloom.net

3   Dominique Christian, *A la recherche du sens dans l'Entreprise ... Compter, raconter? La Stratégie du récit*, Paris: Maxima, 1999. According to his publisher, Christian, a "philosopher by training and a doctor in communications science ... developed the first computer-assisted storytelling system for the business world."

4   See, for example, "Le Management de l'intelligence collective: Intranet/extranet, messagerie, gestion de projet"; available at www.jpmconsulting.fr

5   Stephen Denning, *The Leader's Guide to Storytelling: Mastering the Art and Discipline of Business Narrative*, San Francisco: Jossey-Bass, 2005, p. 5.

6   Joseph Grenny, "Silence Kills. Exploding Shuttles, Media Meltdowns and Health Care Disasters. What's The Underlying Cause?," 2003; available at www.executiveforum.net

7   Cited by Priya Jestin, "Silence Can Kill (Your Project)," Project Management Source, February 15, 2007; available at www.projectmanagementsource.com

8   Leslie A. Perlow, "Is Silence Killing Your Company?," *Harvard Business Review*, 81: 5, May 2003.

9   Ibid.

10 Ibid.

11 Bernard Girard, *Histoire des theories du management en France du début de la revolution industrielle au lendemain de la Première Guerre Mondiale*; available at www.bernardgirard.com

12 Louis Reybaud, *Etudes sur le régime des manufactures: conditions des ouvriers en soie*, Paris: Michel Lévy, 1859.

13 Cited in ibid.

14 On this point, the reader is referred to Luc Boltanski and Eve Chiapello's indispensable *The New Spirit of Capitalism*, trans. Gregory Elliott, London and New York: Verso, 2005.

15 Cited by Marie-Victoire Louis, *Le Droit de cuissage: France 1860–1930*, Paris: Editions ouvrières, 1994, Chapter VII, "Le Silence des femmes."

16 Elizabeth Wolfe Morrison and Frances J. Milliken, "Organizational Silence: A Barrier to Change and Development in a Pluralistic World," *The Academy of Management Review*, 25: 2, October 2000.

17 David M. Boje, "Storytelling Practice and the Narrative–Antenarrative Debate," February 2005; available at http://peaceaware.com

18 Richard Lacayo and Amanda Riple, "The Whistle-Blowers," *Time*, December 22, 2002; available at http://foi.missouri.edu

19 Nicole Giroux, "Vers une narrativité reflexive?," in Eddie Soulier, ed., *Le Storytelling: Concepts, outils et applications*, Paris: Hermès Sciences Publications, 2006, p. 41.

20 Ibid.

21 David M. Boje, "The Storytelling Organization: A Study of Storytelling Performance in an Office-Supply Firm," *Administrative Science Quarterly*, 36: 1, March 1991; available at http://business.nmsu.edu

22 Thierry Boudès, "Des Récits du management au management des récits: pourquoi les gestionnaires font-ils tant d'histoires?," *Les Echos de la recherche*, ESCP, 6, March 2001.

23 Ibid.

24 Stephen Denning, *Squirrel Inc: A Fable of Leadership through Storytelling*, San Francisco: Jossey-Bass, 2004. See also Stephen Denning, *The Leader's Guide to Storytelling: Mastering the Art and Discipline of Business Narrative*, San Francisco: Jossey-Bass, 2005.

25 Lucy Kellaway, "Once Upon A Time, We Had Managers, Not Storytellers," *Financial Times*, May 10, 2004.

26 Evelyn Clark, *Around the Corporate Campfire: How Great Leaders Use Stories to Inspire Success*, Sevierville: Insight Publishing Company, 2004.

27 "Raconte-moi une histoire...," *Stratégies*, 1369, May 12, 2005.

28 Ibid.
29 Sonia Mabrouk, "Il était une fois ... le storytelling," *Jeune Afrique*, April 9, 2006.
30 Kellaway, "Once Upon A Time, We Had Managers, Not Storytellers."
31 Rosabeth Moss Kanter, *On the Frontiers of Management*, Boston: Harvard Business School Press, 1997.
32 Michel Foucault, *The Order of Things: An Archaeology of the Human Sciences*, London: Routledge, 1989, p. xv.
33 Ibid., p. xvi.
34 Vladimir Propp, *Morphology of the Folk Tale*, trans. Lawrence Scott, Bloomington: Indiana University Press, 1958.
35 Cited by John Gaynard, "Storytelling: le management des connaissances et de l'innovation à travers des récits, des contes, et des histoires"; available at www.syre.com; see also Denning, *Squirrel Inc.*
36 David Greatbatch and Timothy Clark, *Management Speak: Why We Believe What Management Gurus Tell Us*, New York: Routledge, 2005.
37 See Kama Kamand, *La Nuit des griots*, Paris: Présence Africaine, 1996; Isabelle Leymarie, *Les Griots wolof du Sénégal*, Paris: Maisonneuve et Larose, 1999.
38 Denning, *Squirrel Inc.*
39 Greatbatch and Clark, *Management Speak*, p. 5.
40 Andrzej Huczynski, *Management Gurus: What Makes Them and How to Become One*, London: Routledge, 1993, p. 38.
41 Greatbatch and Clark, *Management Speak*, pp. 9–10.
42 Ibid., p. 11.
43 Ibid., pp. 7–8
44 Ibid., p. 8.
45 Huczynski, *Management Gurus*; cf. Timothy Clark and Graeme Salaman, "The Management Guru as Organizational Witchdoctor," *Organization*, 3: 1, pp. 85–107.
46 Greatbatch and Clark, *Management Speak*, pp. 36–7.
47 Ibid., p. 38.
48 Ibid., p. 112.
49 Timothy Clark and Graeme Salaman, "Telling Tales: Management Gurus, Narratives and the Construction of Managerial Identity," *Journal of Management Studies*, 35, 1998.
50 Annette Simmons, *The Story Factor: Inspiration, Influence, and Persuasion Through the Art of Storytelling*, New York: Basic Books, revised edition, 2006, p. 3.
51 Roland Barthes, "Dominici, or The Triumph of Literature," in *Mythologies*, trans. Annette Lavers, London: Paladin, 1972, p. 63.
52 Cited by Evelyn Clark, "It's Time For Storytelling, a Proven Management Tool," January 1, 2006; available at www.corpstory.com
53 Paul Corrigan, *Shakespeare on Management*, Dover: Kogan Page, 1999.
54 Robert A. Brawer, *Fictions of Business: Insights on Management from Great Literature*, New York: Wiley, 1998.
55 Yiannis Gabriel, ed., *Myths, Stories, and Organizations*, New York: Oxford University Press, 2004, p. 6.

3 The New "Fiction Economy"

1 Ashim Ahluwalia, introduction to the documentary *John & Jane* (Future East Film, Bombay); available at www.belinale.de
2 Ibid.

3   John Ribeiro, "Cultural Training Moves Offshore," *IDG News Service*, August 22, 2005; available at www.itworld.com (IDG is a news agency providing information about information technologies.)

4   Ibid.

5   Cited by Nanditta Chibber and Abhilash Ojha, "Inde: les artistes fascinés par les téléopérateurs," *Business Standard* (Bombay), February 6, 2007; available at http://voyageavenir.blogspot.com

6   Ribiero, "Cultural Training Moves Offshore."

7   Amelia Gentleman, "Hi, It's Bollywood Calling," *Observer*, May 21, 2006.

8   Joseph Confavreux, "L'Inde à grande vitesse (2/5). Jeunes Indiens travaillant pour l'Occident: une acculturation sur place?," France-Culture, March 20, 2007; available at www.radiofrance.fr

9   Radhika Chadha, "*John & Jane* and Strategy Mutation," *Hindu Business Line*, August 24, 2006.

10   Cameron Bailey, in the Catalogue of the International Film Festival, Toronto, September 2005.

11   Gentleman, "Hi, It's Bollywood Calling."

12   Ibid.

13   Bailey, Catalogue of the International Film Festival, Toronto.

14   Luc Boltanski and Eve Chiapello, *The New Spirit of Capitalism*, trans. Gregory Elliott, London and New York: Verso, 2005, pp. 459–60, emphasis added.

15   Ibid., p. 461, emphasis added.

16   Ibid., pp. 8, 5.

17   Ibid., p. 58.

18   Richard Sennett, *The Corrosion of Character: The Personal Consequences of Work in the New Capitalism*, New York: W. W. Norton and Co., 1998, p. 111.

19   Ibid., citing Charles N. Darrah, *Learning at Work: An Exploration in Industrial Ethnography*, New York: Garland Publishing, 1996, p. 27.

20   Ibid., p. 113, citing Laurie Graham, *On the Line at Subaru-Isuzu: The Japanese Model and the American Worker*, Ithaca: Cornell University Press, 1995, p. 108.

21   Ibid., p. 114.

22   Ibid.

23   Nigel Thrift, *Knowing Capitalism*, London: Sage, 2004, p. 121.

24   Boltanski and Chiapello, *The New Spirit of Capitalism*, p. 459.

25   Ibid., pp. 459–60.

26   Eva Illouz, *Cold Intimacies: The Making of Emotional Capitalism*, Cambridge: Polity, 2007, p. 108.

27   Boltanski and Chiapello, *The New Sprit of Capitalism*, p. 59.

28   Don DeLillo, *Players*, London: Vintage, 1991, p. 18.

29   Ibid.

30   Ibid., p. 42.

31   Ibid., pp. 18–19.

32   Thomas Peters and Robert Waterman, *In Search of Excellence*, New York: Harper and Row, 1982, p. 11.

33   Ibid., p. 19.

34   Ibid.

35   Delillo, *Players*, pp. 43–4.

36   Richard Sennett, "Récits au temps de la précarité," *Le Monde*, May 5, 2006.

37   Ibid.

38   Eddie Soulier, ed., *Le Storytelling: Concepts, outils et applications*, Paris: Hermès Sciences Publications, 2006, pp. 339–59.

39   Dominique Christian, *A la recherche du sens dans l'Entreprise... Compter, raconter? La Stratégie du récit*, Paris: Maxima, 1999.

40   Louis Utichelle, "The Downsizing of America," *New York Times*, May 3, 1996, p. 7–8, cited by Sennett, *The Corrosion of Character*, p. 22.

41   Yves-Frédéric Livian, "La Gestion comme récit. Petite introduction à une narratologie de certains thèmes de gestion des resources humaines," *Gérer et comprendre*, 70, December 2002, pp. 41–8.

42   Soulier, ed., *Le Storytelling*, pp. 339–59.

43   Livian, "La Gestion comme récit."

44   Italo Calvino, *Six Memos for the Next Millennium*, London: Vintage, 2006.

4 The Mutant Companies of New-Age Capitalism

1   Eddie Soulier, ed., *Le Storytelling: Concepts, outils et applications*, Paris: Hermès Sciences Publications, 2006, p. 353.

2   Ibid.

3   Eddie Soulier, "Proposition de thèses, Université de technologie de Troyes"; available at www.utt.fr

4   Soulier, *Le Storytelling*, pp. 339–59.

5   Ibid., pp. 17–22. The volume edited by Eddie Soulier contains a rich bibliography on storytelling. See in particular John Seely Brown, Stephen Denning, Katalina Groh, and Laurence Prusak, *Storytelling in Organizations: Why Storytelling is Transforming 21st Century Organizations and Management*, Oxford: Elvesier, 2004; John Seely Brown and Paul Duguid, *The Social Life of Information*, Boston: Harvard Business School Press, 2000; Stephen Denning, *The Springboard: How Storytelling Ignites Action In Knowledge-Era Organizations*, Oxford: Butterworth-Heinemann, 2000.

6   Jeremy Rifkin, *The Age of Access: The New Culture of Hypercapitalism Where All of Life is a Paid-For Experience*, New York: J. P. Taucher and Putmann, 2000.

7   James B. Twitchell, *Branded Nation: The Marketing of Megachurch, College Inc., and Museumworld*, New York: Simon and Schuster, 2004.

8   David M. Boje, "Storytelling Practice and the Narrative–Antenarrative Debate," February 2005; available at http://peaceaware.com

9   Ibid.

10   Figures taken from Alex Gibney's documentary, *The Smartest Guys in the Room* (2005).

11   Bethany McLean and Peter Elkind, *The Smartest Guys in the Room: The Amazing Rise and Fall of Enron*, New York: Portfolio, 2004.

12   Quoted from Gibney's film, *The Smartest Guys in the Room*.

13   Ibid.

14   David M. Boje, Carolyn L. Gardner, and William L. Smith, "(Mis)using Numbers in the Enron story," *Organizational Research Methods*, 9: 4, 2006.

15   Richard Sennett, *The Culture of the New Capitalism*, New Haven and London: Yale University Press, 2006, p. 40.

16   Nigel Thrift, *Knowing Capitalism*, London: Sage, 2004, p. 122.

17   Alicia Korten and Karen Dietz, "Who Said Money is Everything? Story is the New Currency in Financial Management," in Lori Silverman, ed., *Wake Me Up When the Data Is Over*, San Francisco: Jossey-Bass, 2006, p. 7.

18   Sennett, *The Culture of the New Capitalism*, p. 40.

19   Cited Alex Gibney's film, *The Smartest Guys in the Room*.

5 Turning Politics Into A Story

1   Maggie Downs, "The Hug Becomes a TV Ad for Bush," *The Enquirer*, October 20, 2004.
2   Eric Boehlert, "The TV Ad that Put Bush Over the Top," *Salon*, November 5, 2004.
3   Ibid.
4   The commercial can be seen at www.youtube.com
5   Susan Allen, "Ad Analysis," Political Advertising Resource Center, October 19, 2004; available at www.umdparc.org
6   Boehlert, "The TV Ad that Put Bush Over the Top."
7   Ibid.
8   Cited in ibid.
9   Downs, "The Hug Becomes a TV Ad for Bush."
10 Francesca Polletta, *It Was Like a Fever: Storytelling in Protest and Politics*, Chicago: University of Chicago Press, 2006, p. ix.
11 John Anthony Maltese, *Spin Control: The White House Office of Communications and the Management of Presidential News*, Chapel Hill: University of North Carolina Press, 1994, p. 199.
12 Cited by Polletta, *It Was Like a Fever*, p. vii.
13 Ibid., p. viii.
14 Cited in Nina J. Easton, Michael Kranish, Patrick Healy, Glen Johnson, Anne E. Kornblut, and Brian Mooney, "On the Trail of Kerry's Failed Dream," *Boston Globe*, November 14, 2004.
15 James Carville and Paul Begala, *Buck Up, Suck Up ... and Come Back When You Foul Up: 12 Winning Secrets from the War Room*, New York: Simon and Schuster, 2002, p. 108.
16 Seth Godin, *All Marketers Are Liars: The Power of Telling Authentic Stories in a Low-Trust World*, New York: Portfolio, 2005, pp. 80–1.
17 Dana Thomas, "The Last Word: James Carville Dissecting the Democrats (Interview)," *Newsweek*, October 30, 2006.
18 William Safire, "The Way We Live Now," *New York Times*, December 5, 2004.
19 Ibid.
20 "Meet the Press," *Newsbusters*, October 30, 2005.
21 Carville and Begala, *Buck Up, Suck Up*, p. 109.
22 Evan Cornog, *The Power and the Story: How the Crafted Presidential Narrative has Determined Political Success from George Washington to George W. Bush*, New York: Penguin Press, 2004, p. 1.
23 Ibid., p. 5.
24 Ibid., p. 2.
25 Ibid., p. 274.
26 See, in particular, John Ford's film *The Young Mister Lincoln* (1939).
27 Cf. Cornog, *The Power and the Story*, pp. 39–40.
28 Jeffrey K. Tulis, *The Rhetorical Presidency*, Princeton: Princeton University Press, 1987, p. 95.
29 Peter Brooks, "Stories Abounding," *Chronicle of Higher Education*, November 11, 2001.
30 Serge Halimi, *Le Grand bond en arrière: Comment l'ordre liberal s'Est imposé au monde*, Paris: Fayard, 2006.
31 www.infoplease.com/t/hist/state-of-the-union/198.html
32 www.infoplease.com/t/hist/state-of-the-union/220.html
33 Carville and Begala, *Buck Up, Suck Up*, p. 109.
34 Brooks, "Stories Abounding."
35 Cited by Maltese, *Spin Control*, p. 238.

36 Bill Clinton, *My Life*, New York: Knopf, 2004, p. 16.
37 Ibid., p. 957.
38 Maltese, *Spin Control*, pp. 238–9.
39 Godin, *All Marketers Are Liars*, p. 80.
40 Maltese, *Spin Control*, pp. 238–9.
41 Richard Rose, *The Postmodern President: The White House Meets the World*, Chatham: Chatham House, 1988, Chapter 7.
42 Michel Foucault, "The Order of Discourse," trans. Ian McLeod, in Robert Young, ed., *Untying the Text: A Post-Structuralist Reader*, London: Routledge and Kegan Paul, 1981, p. 62.
43 Richard Nixon, *The Memoirs of Richard Nixon*, New York: Grosset and Dunlap, 1978, p. 354.
44 Cited by Maltese, *Spin Control*, p. 192.
45 Cited ibid.
46 Ibid., p. 198.
47 Cited ibid., p. 215.
48 Ibid., p. 199.
49 Cornog, *The Power and the Story*, p. 67.
50 Ibid., p. 91.
51 Tulis, *The Rhetorical Presidency*, p. 238.
52 Cornog, *The Power and the Story*, pp. 250–1.
53 Ira Chesnus, "Karl Rove's Scheherazade Strategy," July 7, 2006; available at www. tomdispatch.com
54 Ibid.
55 *Le Monde*, August 15, 2007.

6 *Telling War Stories*

1   Steve Silberman, "The War Room," *Wired*, September 2004.
2   Tim Lenoir and Henry Lowood, "Theaters of War: the military-entertainment complex," Stanford University, November 21, 2002; available at www.stanford.edu
3   Ellen Herman, "Project Camelot and the Career of Cold War Psychology," in Christopher Simpson, ed., *Universities and Empire: Money and Politics in the Social Sciences during the Cold War*, New York: New Press, 1998, p. 118.
4   Ed Halter, "War Games: New Media Finds its Place in the New World Order," *Village Voice*, November 13–19, 2002.
5   J. C. Herz, "At Play, It Takes the Army to Save a Village," *New York Times*, February 3, 2000.
6   Nick Gillette, "Learning to Fight," *Guardian*, June 17, 2004.
7   US Congress, Office of Technology Assessment, *After the Cold War: Living with Lower Defense Spending (Summary)*, OTA-ITE-525, Washington, DC, February 1992, cited by Sharon Ghamari-Tabrizi, "The Convergence of the Pentagon and Hollywood," in Lauren Rabinovitz and Abraham Geil, eds, *Memory Bytes: History, Technology and Digital Culture*, Durham, NC: Duke University Press, p. 153.
8   Ibid.
9   Ibid., p. 155.
10 Herz, "At Play, It Takes the Army to Save a Village."
11 Ghamari-Tabrizi, "The Convergence of the Pentagon and Hollywood," p. 153.
12 Cited ibid., p. 155.

13 Herz, "At Play, It Takes the Army to Save a Village."
14 Paul Virilio, *War and Cinema: The Logistics of Perception*, trans. Patrick Camiller, London: Verso, 1989, p. 9.
15 Paul Virilio, *Guerre et cinema. Logistique de la perception*, Paris: Cahiers du cinema, revised expanded edition, 1991.
16 Ghamari-Tabrizi, "The Convergence of the Pentagon and Hollywood," p. 156.
17 Ibid., p. 151.
18 Ibid.
19 Ibid., p. 159.
20 Ibid., p. 160.
21 Silberman, "The War Room."
22 Karen Kaplan, "Army, USC Join Forces for Virtual Research," *Los Angeles Times*, August 18, 1999.
23 Ghamari-Tabrizi, "The Convergence of the Pentagon and Hollywood," pp. 159–60.
24 Ibid., p. 159.
25 Maurice Ronai, "Hollywood et le Pentagone coopèrent dans les effets spéciaux et les techniques de simulation," *Le Débat stratégique*, CIRPES, 46, September 1999.
26 Silberman, "The War Game."
27 Ronai, "Hollywood et le Pentagone."
28 Margaret Thomas Kelso, Peter Weyhrauch, and Joseph Bates, "Dramatic Presence," *Presence* 2: 1, Winter 1993.
29 Cited by Ghamari-Tabrizi, "The Convergence of the Pentagon and Hollywood," p. 162.
30 Michael Duffy, Tim McGirk, and Aparisim Ghosh, "The Ghosts of Haditha," *Time Magazine*, June 4, 2006.
31 Ghamari-Tabrizi, "The Convergence of the Pentagon and Hollywood," p. 169.
32 Cited by James Verini, "War Games, " *Guardian*, April 19, 2005.
33 See Salon.com, October 4, 2002.
34 Cited by Silberman, "The War Room."
35 Heather Chaplin and Aaron Ruby, *Smartbomb: The Quest for Art, Entertainment, and Big Bucks in the Videogame Revolution*, Chapel Hill: Algonquin Books, 2005.
36 Cited by Pat Kane, "Toy Soldiers," *Guardian*, December 1, 2005.
37 Steve O'Hagan, "Recruitment Hard Drive," *Guardian*, June 19, 2004.
38 Larry Gordon, "Virtual War, Real Healing," *Los Angeles Times*, February 9, 2007.
39 Verini, "War Games."
40 Gordon, "Virtual War, Real Healing."
41 Ibid.
42 Jean-Michel Valentin, *Hollywood, le Pentagone et Washington: Les Trois auteurs d'une stratégie globale*, Paris: Autrement, 2003, p. 107.
43 Don Delillo, *Libra*, London: Penguin, 1991, pp. 50, 78, 146–7, 50.
44 Samuel Blumenfeld, "Le Pentagone et la CIA enrôlent Hollywood," *Le Monde*, July 27, 2002.
45 Lenoir and Lowood, "Theaters of War."
46 Ronai, "Hollywood et le Pentagone."
47 Slavoj Žižek, "The Depraved Heroes of *24* are the Himmlers of Hollywood," *Guardian*, January 10, 2006. The reference is to a phrase from Milan Kundera, *Testaments Betrayed*, trans. Linda Asher, London: Faber & Faber, 2004, p. 6.
48 Cited by Colin Freeze, "What Would Jack Bauer Do? Canadian Jurist Prompts International Justice Panel to Debate TV Drama *24*'s Use of Torture," *Globe and Mail* (Ottawa), June 20, 2007.

7 The Propaganda Empire

1   Ron Suskind, "Faith, Certainty and the Presidency of George W. Bush," *New York Times Magazine*, October 17, 2004.

2   Marc Bloch, *The Royal Touch: Sacred Monarchy and Scrofula in England and France*, trans. J. E. Anderson, London: Routledge and Kegan Paul, 1973.

3   Jay Rosen, "The Retreat from Empiricism and Ron Suskind's Intellectual Scoop," *Huffington Post*, July 4, 2007.

4   Cited by Byron Calame, "Scoops, Impact or Glory: What Motivates Reporters?," *New York Times*, December 3, 2006.

5   Rosen, "The Retreat from Empiricism."

6   Eric Boehlert, "Reality-based Reporting," 2004; available at http://dir.salon.com

7   Ibid.

8   Scott McConnell, "Reconnecting with the Reality-Based Community," *The American Conservative*, October 23, 2006. (This is a review of Anatol Lieven and John Hulsman, *A Vision for America's Role in the World*, New York: Pantheon, 2006.)

9   Edward Bernays, *Propaganda*, New York: Ig Publishing, 2005; introduction by Mark Crispin Miller. The book is not well known in Europe. Thanks to a stroke of good fortune, a French translation was published in October 2007 by Zones, with a long critical introduction by Normand Baillargeon.

10   Bernays, *Propaganda*, p. 122. The reference is to the first trans-Atlantic cable laid in 1866; it allowed telegraphic communications between Europe and the US.

11   Ibid., p. 50, citing an article quoted in Funk and Wagnall's Dictionary.

12   Ibid., p. 39.

13   Serge Chakotin, *The Rape of the Masses: The Psychology of Totalitarian Political Propaganda*, New York: Haskell House Publishers Ltd, 1971, p. 91.

14   See Edward S. Harmann and Noam Chomsky, *Manufacturing Consent: The Political Economy of the Mass Media*, London: Vintage, 1998; Noam Chomsky, *Media Control: The Spectacular Achievement of Propaganda*, New York: Seven Stories Press, 2002; Victor Klemperer, *The Language of the Third Reich: LTI. Lingua Tertii Imperii*, London: Continuum, 2006; Jacques Ellul, *Histoire de la propaganda*, Paris: PUF, Collecton "Que sais-je?," 1967; Philippe Breton, *La Parole manipulée*, Paris: La Découverte, 1998; André Schriffin, *Le Contrôle de la parole*, Paris: La Fabrique, 2005; Eric Hazan, *LQR: La Propagande du quotidian*, Paris: Raisons d'agir, 2006.

15   I refer the reader, if I may, to the three issues of the journal *Autodafé* (Paris: Denoël, 2001, 2002, and 2003), and my own *Tombeau de la fiction* (Paris: Denoël, 1999) and *Verbicide: Du bon usage des cerveaux humains disponibles* (Arles: Actes Sud, 2006).

16   Bernays, *Propaganda*, p. 40

17   Frank Rich, *The Greatest Story Ever Sold: The Decline and Fall of Truth in Bush's America*, New York: Penguin, 2006, pp. 2–3.

18   Walter Benjamin, "The Storyteller," trans. Harry Zohn, in *Selected Writings, Volume 3: 1935–1938*, Cambridge, MA: Belknap Press of Harvard University Press, 2002, pp. 147–8.

19   Seth Godin, *All Marketers Are Liars: The Power of Telling Authentic Stories in a Low-Trust World*, New York: Portfolio, 2005, pp. 141–2, 140.

20   Ibid., pp. 140–1.

21   "Why Fox News is an Industry Joke, Or Welcome to Infotainment Tonight!" (2004); available at www.turnoffyourtv.com.

22   Godin, *All Marketers Are Liars*, p. 141.

23   John. S. Carroll, "The Wolf in Reporter's Clothing: The Rise of Pseudo-Journalism in America," *Los Angeles Times*, May 6, 2004.

24   Michael Massing, "The End of News?," *New York Review of Books*, December 1, 2005.
25   Rich, *The Greatest Story*, p. 166.
26   Ibid., p. 170.
27   Gardiner Harris, "Surgeon General Sees 4-Year Term as Compromised," *New York Times*, July 11, 2007.
28   *Le Monde*, July 11, 2007.
29   Rich, *The Greatest Story*, p. 171.
30   Ibid., p. 179.
31   Cited by Massing, "The End of News?"
32   Mark Mazzetti and Borzou Daragahi, "US Military Covertly Pays to Run Stories in Iraqi Press," *Los Angeles Times*, November 30, 2005.
33   Ibid.
34   Ibid.
35   David Blaine, *Mysterious Stranger: A Book of Magic*, New York: Villard Books, 2002.
36   Michael Tomasky, "How Democrats Should Talk," *New York Review of Books*, May 31, 2007.
37   Rich, *The Greatest Story*, p. 89.
38   Ibid., p. 57.
39   Ibid.
40   Cited by Sheldon Rampton and John Stauba, "How to Sell a War," *In These Times*, August 4, 2003; available at www.frankwbaker.com
41   Cited by Nancy Snow, *Information War: American Propaganda, Free Speech, and Opinion Control since 9/11*, New York: Seven Stories Press, 2003, pp. 84–5.
42   *Good Morning America*, ABC News, December 14, 2001, cited at www.fpif.org
43   Cited by Snow, *Information War*, p. 85.
44   Ibid., p. 86.
45   Charlotte Beers, "Public Diplomacy After September 11: Remarks to the National Press Club," Washington DC, December 18, 2002; available at www.state.gov
46   Snow, *Information War*, p. 86.
47   Ibid.
48   Ibid.
49   Boehlert, "Reality-based Reporting."
50   Massing, "The End of News?"
51   Jean Lacroix, "De la démocratie libérale à la démocratie massive," *Esprit*, March 1946.
52   Bernays, *Propaganda*, p. 49.
53   The whole address can be consulted at www.whitehouse.gov
54   Slavoj Žižek, "New Yorkers Face the Fire in the Minds of Men," *Guardian*, September 11, 2006.
55   James H. Billington, *Fire in the Minds of Men: Origins of the Revolutionary Faith*, New York: Basic Books, 1980, p. 3.
56   Don DeLillo, "In the Ruins of the Future," *Harper's Magazine*, December 2001, p. 33.
57   Jeffrey C. Alexander, "From the Depths of Despair: Performance, Counter-performance and 'September 11,'" *Sociological Theory*, 22: 1, March 2004.
58   See Peter Sloterdijk, *Die Sonne und der Tod: Dialogische Untersuchungern*, Frankfurt: Suhrkamp, 2002.
59   Gabriel Tarde, *Les Lois de l'imitation*, Paris: Kimé, 1993 (first published in 1895).
60   Lori L. Silverman, *Wake Me Up When the Data Is Over*, San Francisco: Jossey-Bass, 2006, p. xvii.

Afterword: Obama in Fabula

1   Sharon Begley, "Heard Any Good Stories Lately?," *Newsweek*, September 22, 2008; available at http://www.newsweek.com
2   *Newsweek*, May 2, 2008.
3   *New York Times*, February 24, 2008.
4   *Guardian*, May 5, 2008.
5   ABC News, April 29, 2008.
6   Norman Mailer, "Superman Comes to the Supermarket," *Esquire*, November 1960.
7   *Time Magazine*, September 10, 2008.
8   *Wired*, September 3, 2008.
9   Joann Wypijewski, "Beauty and the Beast," *The Nation*, September 10, 2008.
10 Jonathan Freedman, "From West Wing to the Real Thing," *Guardian*, February 21, 2008.
11 Ben Wallace-Wells, "Obama's Narrator," *New York Times Magazine*, April 1, 2007.
12 *Washington Post*, January 28, 2008.
13 Cited on streetprophet.com
14 Barack Obama, *Dreams from My Father: A Story of Race and Inheritance*, Edinburgh: Canongate, 2007, p. 203.
15 Barack Obama, *The Audacity of Hope: Thoughts on Reclaiming the American Dream*, Edinburgh: Canongate, 2007, p. 123.
16 Ibid., p. 124.
17 Ibid., p. 127.
18 Obama, *Dreams from My Father*, pp. xv–xvi.
19 Ibid., p. 82.
20 Ibid., pp. 193, 85.
21 David Brooks, "Run, Barack, Run," *New York Times*, October 19, 2006.
22 Obama, *Dreams from My Father*, p. 198.